DECISIONS AT
YALTA

DECISIONS AT YALTA

An Appraisal of Summit Diplomacy

Russell D. Buhite

SR *Scholarly Resources Inc.*
Wilmington, Delaware

The paper used in this publication meets the minimum requirements of the American National Standard for permanence of
paper for printed library materials, Z39.48, 1984.

© 1986 Scholarly Resources Inc.
All rights reserved
First published 1986
Printed and bound in the United States of America

Scholarly Resources Inc.
104 Greenhill Avenue
Wilmington, Delaware 19805-1897

Library of Congress Cataloging-in-Publication Data

Buhite, Russell D.
    Decisions at Yalta.

    Bibliography: p.
    Includes index.
    1. Yalta Conference (1945)   2. World politics—
1945–   . 3. World War, 1939–1945—Peace. I. Title.
D734.C7   1945zl   940.53′14   86-13779
ISBN 0-8420-2256-2 (alk. paper)
ISBN 0-8420-2268-6 (pbk.: alk. paper)

Acknowledgments

I am obliged to acknowledge the aid and assistance of a number of individuals in the completion of this work. My primary debt is to the nameless freshman in a class of 500 who suggested that I do a book on Yalta. I hope he earned an "A." Richard Hopper, acquisitions editor for Scholarly Resources, expressed early interest in the project and encouraged me to complete the study and submit it for publication. To Carolyn Travers, the project editor, and to others on the editorial staff, I am grateful for the elimination of stylistic slips and the various and sundry errors that exist in any manuscript. My research assistant, Garth Todd, did yeoman work in gathering both manuscript and secondary materials for my use. The staff at the Franklin D. Roosevelt Library proved most cooperative and helpful during my stay there in the summer of 1984, a stay made possible by a grant from the Four Freedoms Foundation of the Roosevelt Library. Paul Varg provided a careful reading of the manuscript and gave me the benefit of his ideas, while my colleague Henry Tobias discussed a number of points of interpretation with me. As she has done in the past, Martha Penisten, administrative secretary at the university's History Department, generously interrupted her busy schedule to type the manuscript. Finally, my wife Mary—helpmate, companion, and best friend—gave support that only she could provide, or permit. That the above have incurred no responsibility for any errors of fact or interpretation existing in the book will not prevent my sharing the blame with them.

For Mike

Contents

Introduction

This book is designed primarily for students in American history courses as well as for the lay reader who may be interested in an interpretive account of one of this century's most important and controversial summit conferences. It is not intended to be an exhaustive or definitive study of the subject based on new archival research, although it does include information not previously available. It places Yalta within the context of détente and emphasizes that in the two main periods during which the United States and the Soviet Union pursued a détente relationship such an asymmetry of views existed that avoiding serious discord became virtually impossible.

A working definition of the term détente and a brief account of its meaning to American and Soviet policymakers historically are essential to an understanding of the divergent approaches and expectations at Yalta. Without belaboring the issue, it can simply be said that détente is a method or process that states may use to put aside differences and improve relations in the interest of avoiding conflict among them. In the case of the United States and the Soviet Union, it has involved the construction of a network of agreements, either to meet a common objective, as during World War II when no real entente cordiale developed, or, as in the last twenty years, to avoid nuclear holocaust.

For the Soviet Union, détente arose out of the concept of coexistence, a foreign policy approach that had its origins in the early postrevolutionary period. Although Marxist-Leninist ideology postulated that the transition to socialism would require war or violent revolution, Soviet leaders in the 1920s, realizing the comparative weakness of the new Soviet state, decided that they had to avoid war with the capitalist nations in the short term. The way to do this was to concentrate on increasing Soviet strength, while downplaying the promotion of international communism. During the World War II era the Soviets made distinctions among the capitalist nations. There were those virulently aggressive and expansionist states like Germany, Japan, and Italy that posed an immediate threat to the Soviet Union and the democracies that remained dangerous in the long run but with whom they could ally in addressing the present danger. Thus Premier Joseph Stalin adapted ideology to the interest of Soviet security, and he deemphasized its importance in his relations with the Western allies. At Yalta he pursued a policy of détente with the United States and Great Britain, but he did so without altering, to any significant degree, the basic aims and objectives of the Soviet Union.

From the American perspective, Yalta provided the opportunity to codify the wartime community of interest in a set of agreements that would satisfy the needs of the major powers, establish a mechanism within the United Nations for protecting the interests of the smaller nations, and promote the general peace. Through the Declaration on Liberated Europe and the emphasis on reorganization of the government of Poland, President Franklin D. Roosevelt and Prime Minister Winston Churchill advanced their expectations that liberal democratic, as well as basic human, values would be observed. Roosevelt and other members of the U.S. delegation had high hopes for the ideals expressed in the Yalta accords, despite their willingness to concede a sphere of influence in Eastern Europe to the Soviet Union.

American dreams were dashed because the détente Stalin formalized at Yalta differed substantially from that of his Western allies. The United Nations meant nothing to him except as a show of cooperation with his U.S. ally to secure concessions in other areas of negotiation at the Crimean meeting and to provide an opening wedge for subsequent loans from the United States. Nor did he envision the Declaration on Liberated Europe as serving to prevent Soviet freedom of action in Eastern Europe. Indeed, Stalin firmly believed that the United States and Great Britain should guarantee Soviet territorial aspirations, an issue that he raised on numerous occasions during the war, even while German troops occupied a large sector of Soviet territory. Despite Stalin's wartime deemphasis of the issue, he did not share Roosevelt's notion that ideology would play a minimal role in the future Soviet-American relationship, looking ahead instead to the advancement of Soviet influence in Western Europe through Communist parties then under Moscow's control. Finally, détente meant a solution to the Soviets' long-standing Japan problem through an arrangement in which they would sell their military services to the United States, thereby gaining concessions and bases in China and the right to participate in the disposition of Japanese property and territory.

To see Yalta in proper perspective is to view it as the first effort to codify détente, the second coming in the 1970s. From the Soviet side, the second attempt had its origins in Nikita Khrushchev's speech to the Twentieth Party Congress in 1956. In addition to detailing many of Stalin's crimes, the new Soviet leader advanced the proposition that, because nuclear arms made all-out war suicidal for both Socialist and capitalist states, it was necessary to pursue a policy of "peaceful coexistence." The Soviet Union was the only Socialist state when it first developed this policy in the 1920s; now there were several as models for the rest of the world. It would be possible to compete peacefully with the United States to avoid a destructive war, but, at the same time, the Soviets would support wars of national liberation in the Third World. Khrushchev had no doubt that, through the avoidance of war with the United States and through both peaceful and nonpeaceful competition in the Third World, eventually socialism would triumph everywhere.

What Khrushchev had in mind was the simultaneous pursuit of coexistence and expansion. What he got because he chose to support a Third World revolution in the American sphere of influence was a major crisis over Cuba that threatened to blow up the world; more than anything else it pointed out the inherent contradiction in the Soviet approach. The Cuban missile crisis, however, represented a turning point on the road to détente, and thereafter the United States and the Soviet Union moved to establish agreements to improve relations, including the nuclear test ban of 1963. In the 1970s when the foreign policy team of Richard Nixon and Henry Kissinger sought to promote a new international equilibrium, including the People's Republic of China, the result was the second formal effort at Soviet-American détente.

The American motivation for détente in the 1970s arose from the desire to create a policy that would allow the United States to promote world order without bankrupting the nation's economy and further antagonizing public opinion. It provided a way to balance the objectives of U.S. foreign policy with the limited means available in the wake of the Vietnam War. Ingredients of the new approach included ties to China that would create apprehension within the Soviet Union, promises of a most-favored-nation commercial treaty with the Soviets, sale of U.S. technology to the Russians, and a strategic arms limitation agreement. In return the Soviets would be expected to remain relatively quiescent in the Third World and to adhere to provisions of the arms limitation agreement.

Differing interpretations of its meaning also led to the early demise of the 1970s version of détente. American politicians, led by Senator Henry M. Jackson (D-WA), insisted that most-favored-nation treatment be denied the Soviets until they allowed for the large-scale emigration of Jews. Conservatives in both parties began to question the Soviets' commitment to the Helsinki accords of 1975 in which the latter gave assurances of allegiance to certain human rights principles. It became impossible for Kissinger to maintain linkage because too many variables existed in the formulation of U.S. policy. He could not retain control of events regardless of any understanding concluded with General Secretary Leonid Brezhnev.

In the meantime, as at Yalta, the Soviets had their own view of what détente meant. They had no intention of avoiding competition with the United States in the Third World, or of diminishing their ideological effort. Among other moves they subsidized a Cuban intervention in Angola to bring a pro-Soviet government to power in that country, and they gave large-scale backing to Vietnam in its invasion of Cambodia. They interpreted the Helsinki accords as a peace treaty guaranteeing the status quo in Eastern Europe, but they gave short shrift to the human rights part of that agreement. Indeed, the Russians followed up the Helsinki accords with a crackdown on dissidents within the Soviet Union. Most important, they used the period of the 1970s to carry out the largest buildup of military power since the American mobilization in World War II.

Since Yalta was a wartime conference in which military accomplishment affected major political decisions, it is important in introductory remarks to review briefly the state of the war in early 1945. Such a review will demonstrate, among other things, that Yalta took place against a background of Soviet military success in Europe and American success in the Pacific.

Looking first at the European war, the Soviets by February 1945 had reversed the tremendous setbacks of 1941 and 1942, cleared German armies from Russian territory, and moved in force into Eastern Europe. By every measure the Soviets' record was impressive, easily dwarfing the achievements of their Western allies in this theater.

Neither the British nor the Americans, who entered the war in December 1941, provided much assistance during the first eighteen months after the Nazi attack on Russia, thereby requiring that the Soviets meet the German onslaught as best they could. During this period, and later, the Soviets bore the brunt of German military might. In 1941 and 1942, Stalin begged for either a second front in France, a British commitment of roughly thirty divisions to Archangel, or sending British forces to the Southern Front through Iran. The British would not consent to any of these requests, largely because of the unavailability of men and landing craft as well as their unwillingness to risk casualties.

Once the United States entered the war, Anglo-American military planners debated the opening of a second front in Europe with results that were not conducive to strategic advantage at the end of the conflict. The American Joint Chiefs of Staff, led by General George C. Marshall, argued strenuously for a cross-Channel invasion of the coast of France at the earliest in 1942, or in 1943 at the latest. The British would not agree, preferring instead to attack the German heartland with bombing raids and to undertake less risky offensives against the periphery of the German "empire." Consequently, the Western allies opted for an attack in North Africa in November 1942, an offensive that an embittered Stalin saw as not terribly useful in relieving pressure on the Russian front and as evidence of a Western desire to let the Germans and Soviets destroy one another. Repeated promises, and postponements, of a second front in Western Europe did not assuage the Soviets' suspicion. The British and Americans followed the effort in North Africa with further peripheral action by invading Sicily and Italy.

Meanwhile, Soviet armies stopped the German invader in the bloody battle of Stalingrad, which raged from November 1942 to February 1943, lifted the siege of Leningrad in January 1943, and began a major counteroffensive. By the time the Western allies opened the second front in Normandy in June 1944, the Soviets were on the move. Their armies began a drive into the Baltic states, Poland, Hungary, and Romania. From June to September 1944, Soviet forces inflicted nearly 900,000 casualties on the Germans, a figure that exceeded by 200,000 the total number of German troops engaged against General Dwight D. Eisenhower in the west.

In the fall of 1944, Adolf Hitler made a decision about German resistance on the Eastern and Western fronts that had major repercussions at Yalta. He transferred a number of divisions from the Eastern Front to the west, and he sent a large reserve force organized in Germany to the western lines. On December 16 he began a major counteroffensive, in which Marshal Karl von Rundstedt pushed a large "bulge" in Allied lines, thereby forcing Eisenhower's First Army to fall back to the Meuse. This "Battle of the Bulge" constituted a German reinvasion of Belgium and seriously delayed the Allied entry into Germany.

The German offensive induced Eisenhower to appeal for more men and supplies and compelled Western leaders to ask Stalin for second front assistance. Poorly trained youthful recruits from the United States were rushed to the front lines, as were tens of thousands of men from various units scattered around the world. On December 23, President Roosevelt, acting at Eisenhower's behest, sent a message to Stalin inquiring if the Soviet leader would receive U.S. staff officers to discuss coordination of military offensives. Stalin agreed. Churchill followed this request with one of his own regarding the date of a Russian offensive. Stalin told him that the Soviets were waiting for good weather, essentially the same remarks he had made to Ambassador W. Averell Harriman in mid-December, but then told the prime minister that they would begin their offensive by late January. When the American staff officers arrived in Moscow on January 15, Stalin took great delight in telling them that, in spite of bad weather, preparations for the offensive had been accelerated and the offensive had started on January 12. He stressed his reliability as an ally: "We have no treaty but we are comrades. It is proper and also sound selfish policy that we should help each other in times of difficulty. It would be foolish for me to stand aside and let the Germans annihilate you; they would only turn back on me when you were disposed of. Similarly, it is to your interest to do everything possible to keep the Germans from annihilating me."[1]

Stalin's winter offensive proved successful beyond expectation. By the time the Yalta Conference began, Soviet forces had moved across the Vistula River and captured Warsaw; overrun East Prussia, thereby separating it from Germany; moved into upper Silesia; and advanced to within about forty miles of Berlin.

The Soviets thus held Poland in their grasp and were on the verge of capturing Berlin as the Allied leaders sat down to negotiate on Germany and Poland.

Meanwhile, the United States carried on the war against Japan, only marginally aided by its allies. Although the conflict would last until August and there were many bloody battles yet to win, American forces were moving rapidly toward final victory. By February 1945 the United States had achieved domination of the Pacific, the battle for the Philippine island of Leyte in October 1944 signaling a decisive negative turn for the Japanese. American naval and air power extended to China, Taiwan, and the Ryukyus in the south and to Attu Island at the end of the Aleutians in the north. Regular air bombardment of the Japanese home islands took place with the Japanese virtually powerless to stop the attacks. Although Japan had over 1 million men in Manchuria and Korea, perhaps 1 million more in China, and as many as 2 million within Japan proper, its military collapse was imminent. Notwithstanding the unresolved problems within China as the Yalta sessions convened, U.S. officials had every reason to feel confident about the American position in Asia and the Pacific.

Note

[1]Stalin, quoted in Herbert Feis, *Churchill-Roosevelt-Stalin: The War They Waged and the Peace They Sought*, p. 482.

I
Setting and Personalities

Winston Churchill said that if the Allies had looked for ten years they could not have found a worse meeting place than Yalta, and only an adequate supply of whiskey would make a stay there bearable. Why President Franklin D. Roosevelt, a paraplegic dying of cardiovascular disease, and Prime Minister Churchill, then past seventy and with recent physical problems of his own, would travel halfway around the world to meet Stalin in such an improbable spot is a matter that deserves attention.

Agreement to meet at Yalta came after six months of wrangling on the part of Roosevelt, Churchill, and Stalin, the latter of whom was decidedly less anxious for a conference than his Western counterparts. Roosevelt, who already had conferred with Churchill, first suggested the Big Three meeting in a message to Stalin of July 17, urging the Soviet leader to consider traveling to northern Scotland sometime between September 10 and 15. Stalin, who told the president that his involvement in the direction of the Soviet military offensive precluded his leaving Moscow, would have no part in the plan. Roosevelt therefore had to put aside his idea for the time being, but he requested that the Soviet leader keep it in mind because further strategic decisions were necessary, and "such a meeting would help me domestically."[1] The reference to his domestic situation suggests that for Roosevelt political gain, especially his own reelection, was as important as strategic imperatives, at least prior to November 1944.

When it became obvious to the president that a meeting before the election was impossible, he had W. Averell Harriman, U.S. ambassador to Moscow, ask Stalin about conferring in late November somewhere in the Mediterranean. This time Stalin said that his doctors would not permit him to travel because, after his last major trips to Tehran and to the military front, he had become ill and it had taken him a long while to recover. He stated then, and a number of times thereafter, that he would prefer to send Vyacheslav Molotov to a conference, and that the Soviet foreign minister would go anywhere the Allies wished, an offer that in retrospect the Allies should have seized upon. That Stalin did not look well to Harriman when the latter visited him in late September does not gainsay the fact that it was less his health and more his desire to avoid traveling to areas outside his personal control that influenced the Soviet dictator. Harriman's belief that Stalin was using his doctors' advice as an excuse, rather than a reason, for not traveling is demonstrated in the ambassador's only partially facetious suggestion that he should get "some new doctors."

Realizing the difficulty in ever convincing Stalin to leave Soviet territory, Roosevelt apparently intimated to his aide Harry L. Hopkins that he might have to meet with the Soviet leader somewhere along the Black Sea coast. At the time of his remark to Hopkins, the president felt pressured to arrange an early conference because Churchill was going to Moscow in October. Roosevelt believed that, in their bilateral talks, the British and Soviets might reach agreements detrimental to U.S. postwar objectives through some sort of balance-of-power accord. Whatever Roosevelt's exact intentions, Hopkins, more than anyone else, determined the location of the conference by dropping the word to Soviet Ambassador Andrei Gromyko that the president was "anxious to meet Marshal Stalin somewhere in the Black Sea area." Stalin picked this up immediately, and from that moment on he became quite unwilling to consider any other site.

Although Churchill expressed his grudging willingness to convene a conference along the Black Sea coast in late November, in accord with Hopkins's remarks, President Roosevelt quickly disavowed Hopkins and expressed misgivings. He wired Stalin on October 24 that either Athens, Malta, or Cyprus would be a better location and then indicated to Churchill that the Black Sea was not satisfactory because of its distance and poor sanitary conditions. Churchill in reply suggested Jerusalem, to which Stalin could travel by train. As the weeks went by, Roosevelt decided that a conference prior to his inauguration would be difficult to arrange logistically, and events would make it hard for him to leave Washington prior to that time. After January 20 he hoped that Stalin would consent to travel either to one of the Adriatic ports or the Mediterranean. Stalin, however, demurred on all the options, again indicating that his doctors advised against a long journey.

Roosevelt thereupon gave up, deciding that if the Big Three met the conference would have to be held on Soviet territory, probably in the Black Sea area. In a message to Churchill of December 9, 1944, he mentioned Batum or Yalta as possibilities. (Apparently this was the first time anyone had considered Yalta specifically.) On December 23 the president wired Churchill: "If Stalin cannot manage to meet us in the Mediterranean I am prepared to go to the Crimea and have the meeting at Yalta which appears to be the best place available in the Black Sea having the best accommodations ashore and the most promising conditions."[2] The prime minister assented but replied cynically that the president had better secure Stalin's firm agreement lest he come back and say why don't you come on the other four hours and let me entertain you in Moscow!

Having agreed to meet in the Crimea, Churchill then became enthusiastic. For the conference, he suggested the code name ARGONAUT, which the President picked up with alacrity since, as he put it to Churchill, "you and I are direct descendants." Then the prime minister, who wished to meet Roosevelt for preliminary discussion at Malta, became silly: "No more let us falter! From Malta to Yalta! Let nobody alter!" Roosevelt replied that he would stop at Malta on February 1 and would proceed to Yalta "without faltering," thus rebuffing Churchill's plans for a British-American preconference session.

Yalta in early 1945 was not paradise. President Roosevelt sent one of his trusted Secret Service officers, Michael F. Reilly, out to the Crimea in January, and what the agent found would have been disturbing to the traveler most accustomed to primitive conditions. The distance itself was a major problem. Reilly flew from Washington to Bermuda, a 700-mile trip, and then on to the Azores, Casablanca, and finally Naples. From Naples he visited Malta and inspected the harbor where President Roosevelt's ship would dock. From Malta he arranged to fly to Yalta to gauge the difficulty of the flight and to determine the safest route. This was a matter of great importance because the direct route from Malta was over the Dardanelles, which remained under German control; it would be necessary to fly over Athens to Istanbul and then over the Black Sea. For President Roosevelt it would be essential that he fly not only this narrow passageway but also at low altitudes due to his serious heart and blood pressure problems.

Both because of the danger and because Roosevelt did not like to fly, he would have preferred to travel to Yalta by ship. Reilly found the airstrip at Saki quite unsatisfactory. In fact, it was little more than a cow pasture, compounding the danger in getting the president safely to his destination. The other alternative—to transport him by ship across the Black Sea—was not possible because the Germans had mined the sea. To quote the Russian advance agent, "They didn't leave a map." From Saki it was necessary to travel over a rocky, unpaved road by car or jeep some ninety miles to Yalta, which was inaccessible any other way.

Yalta itself was in ruins. The Germans had done their best to destroy the town. Along the road next to the shore were three palaces formerly used as vacation residences by the czars. These palaces, in which the conferees eventually would assemble, were hardly habitable by any standard. They had been stripped of plumbing fixtures, beds, chairs and carpets, kitchen utensils, and stood in an advanced state of filth. They each had only enough bathrooms for the average-sized family, let alone the numerous diplomats and military officers that would be arriving. That the Soviets could restore these palatial structures and make them halfway livable, which they did by simply raiding the contents of the Hotel Metropol in Moscow, is testimony to their efficiency and diligence, not to say their desire to impress their guests with Russian comforts.

Tiring and inconvenient for Prime Minister Churchill, getting to Yalta was a major project for President Roosevelt. He left Washington by train at about 10:45 P.M. on January 22 for Norfolk, Virginia, where he boarded the USS *Quincy* for the trip to Malta. Escorted by three destroyers and a light cruiser, the *Quincy* set a course that would take it near Bermuda, past the Canary Islands, through the Strait of Gibraltar, and into the Mediterranean. During this part of the voyage the president and his advisers were kept in contact with events in Washington and around the world by long-range planes that made regular drops of mail pouches near the *Quincy* which were then fished from the sea. On the evening of January 30 the vessel was near Tangier, and on February 2 it docked at Malta, 4,883 miles from the

Virginia coast. At Malta, Roosevelt left the ship for a tour of the island, which had received heavy bombing over the previous four years. Indeed it had been so devastated that it was nearly impossible for the British, who served as hosts for the military strategists who met there prior to the Yalta sessions, to find meeting places and living quarters for their guests.

Roosevelt remained at Malta, although mostly on board ship, through the evening of February 2, conferring with his Joint Chiefs of Staff and with the Combined Chiefs of Staff, along with Churchill. Afraid that if he and Churchill, who wanted a full-dress, U.S.-British conference, spent any more time together Stalin would believe that his Western allies were ganging up on him, the president boarded his plane at 3:30 A.M. on February 3 for the last leg of his trip to Yalta.

The trip from Malta was neither comfortable nor entirely secure. Equipped with a cage elevator to lift the president on board and a cabin so he could get some sleep on the journey, the DC-3 was forced to fly the entire distance of 1,375 miles at a maximum altitude of 6,000 feet because of Roosevelt's illness and at a top speed of 220 miles per hour, the plane's limit. Five U.S. fighter planes (P-38s) escorted the aircraft from Athens onward. Although the president slept, he did not rest well because the long journey at such a low altitude was regularly punctuated by heaving, bouncing, and turning as the plane flew through the thick clouds. John Kenneth Galbraith later wrote that "those who have flown only in the modern jet cannot know how unpleasant was an ocean crossing in those primitive bucket-seat planes. . . . It was too dark to read, too noisy and too cold to sleep." Never did life "so nearly stand still."[3] To avoid German-controlled territory the plane flew over Athens and then over Turkey and across the Black Sea to Saki. Altogether, discounting the two-hour advance in the clock, the trip took nearly seven hours.

Churchill arrived at Saki twenty minutes after Roosevelt, but the president remained on his plane until Churchill greeted him. The prime minister had left London on January 29 on board a four-engine, U.S.-built Skymaster, along with his daughter and representatives of the British Foreign Office. He arrived in Malta on January 30, fresh and apparently recovered from a slight fever that had worried his physician when they departed, but minus one of his staff planes which had crashed into the Mediterranean

Sea killing all five people aboard. After meeting briefly with Roosevelt on February 2, he flew to Saki, where he was greeted by Foreign Minister Molotov before again seeing the president.

After a brief exchange of pleasantries with Churchill, Molotov and other Soviet officials, as well as Harriman and Secretary of State Edward R. Stettinius, Jr., who had flown on ahead, Roosevelt reviewed an honor guard and then began the automobile trip to Yalta, accompanied by his daughter. Near the landing strip the Russians had set up three huts filled with refreshments—caviar, smoked sturgeon, black bread, butter, cheese, boiled eggs, tea, brandy, and vodka—of which Churchill partook, but the president quickly got into the Packard which the Soviets had furnished him for the ninety-mile journey.

Some measure of the difficulty of this part of the trip was that it took over five hours for the various cars to travel across the bleak, battle-scarred peninsula to Yalta. Every fifty yards or so along the route the Soviets had stationed military sentries, many of them women or young girls with Springfield rifles who regularly saluted the president as he rode by. He saluted back for a while before sliding down in his seat and napping for much of the way. Near the mid-point the Russians had set up another refreshment tent, but Roosevelt remained in the car. From Saki to Simferopol, the Crimean capital, his car traveled over rolling snow-covered land nearly devoid of trees but speckled with the remains of German tanks and railroad equipment. Leaving Simferopol the motorcade went on to Aluskta, an eastern coastal town; wound around the west side of Roman Kosh, a 5,000-foot mountain; and then descended again to the coastal road, passing at dusk through the town of Yalta, whose normal prewar population was 29,000. The president arrived shortly after 6:00 P.M. at Livadia Palace, the U.S. residence and headquarters for the conference, located two miles south of Yalta.

Built between 1910 and 1911 of marble and sandstone. Livadia Palace was a fifty-room structure overlooking the Black Sea some 150 feet below. It once functioned as a summer residence for the seven-member royal family who employed a staff of 1,000 laborers and servants, and following the revolution it served as a sanatorium. An advance American squadron from the USS *Catoctin* had sprayed the palace for lice and other vermin, while Secret Service officials prepared to remove the bugs placed there by the NKVD, the Soviet military intelligence organization. The president's quarters, including the former bedroom of the czar, were located just off the conference hall on the first floor, where all the plenary sessions were to convene. For meetings with advisers, Roosevelt would use the czar's study. Stettinius had a two-room suite, also on the first floor, while General George C. Marshall was given the imperial bedroom on the second floor. There were also adequate rooms for James F. Byrnes, Charles E. Bohlen, presidential aide Edwin "Pa" Watson, Harriman, and Hopkins. The delegates from the State Department, however, had only small rooms, and some of the generals had to sleep five to a room. Only six bathrooms existed to accommodate 215 Americans, with Roosevelt having the only private one.

Varontsov Palace, which became the residence of Prime Minister Churchill and the British delegation, was located approximately ten miles from Livadia. Completed in the mid-nineteenth century, Varontsov was built of diabase stone and combined nineteenth-century Tudor and oriental decors. Churchill had a three-room suite in which a number of his advisers, including Foreign Secretary Anthony Eden, also stayed. The palace had only one-third as many baths as Livadia, thereby causing long lines and accompanying discomfort, and it housed the same kinds of vermin, including bedbugs.

Compared to Roosevelt and Churchill, Stalin had a short and comfortable journey, traveling along the Don River and through Veronezh, Kharkov, and Dnepropetrovsk. He made the 900-mile trip from Moscow on an armored train guarded by troops with antiaircraft guns on flatcars. Stalin arranged to arrive one day late at Yalta, claiming to have been detained by military matters. The Soviet residence, situated nearly equidistant from the British and American headquarters, was at Koreis Villa, a mid-nineteenth century palace once the property of Prince Yusupov, one of the alleged assassins of Rasputin.[4] Having insisted that his Western allies come to him for the conference, Stalin did not take the next step and demand that the meetings be held at Koreis; the plenary sessions, he graciously suggested, should take place at Livadia.

When Stalin arrived on the morning of February 4, Roosevelt, who believed in the manner of a schoolyard adolescent that, if he magnified his differences with a friend, he could placate a potential adversary, sent Ambassador Harriman to arrange a meeting with the Soviet leader prior to the opening of the conference. Harriman met with Molotov, who told him that Stalin would like to meet the president around 4:00 P.M. instead of 3:00

or 3:30 as Roosevelt had planned. As it turned out, Stalin secretly had arranged a meeting with Churchill for 3:00 o'clock, ostensibly to inquire about his comfort but actually to discuss Germany.

The Churchill-Stalin talk focused mainly on Germany's military conditions and the campaign in Italy. Stalin praised the Allied bombing attacks and the damage they had done, especially to the transportation system. He also noted that Germany was short on staples, such as bread and coal, and on the Eastern Front had even begun to throw old men and young boys into battle. To Churchill's query as to the Soviet response should Hitler move to a redoubt in Bavaria or elsewhere, Stalin said his troops would "follow him." In the British map room, Field Marshal Harold Alexander illustrated the Italian campaign, which in turn prompted Stalin to ask Churchill why the Allies did not divert troops into Yugoslavia toward Vienna and Central Europe. Stalin was playing a game since he knew that the British prime minister had long urged Americans to follow such a strategy, a strategy designed to beat the Russians to Central Europe. "It cost him nothing to say this now," Churchill later wrote, but he did not "reproach him" for it.[5]

At 4:00 P.M. on February 4 the front doors of Livadia Palace burst open as American Secret Service men, followed by a group of NKVD officials, escorted the Soviet dictator into the U.S. headquarters. Roosevelt greeted him in his study, a square, ill-lighted room adorned by a couple of paintings, a chandelier filled with odd-sized light bulbs, two plush chairs, a couch, a marble table, and a desk. After a quick exchange of greetings and inquiries about the president's comfort, Roosevelt and Stalin began a one-hour general discussion.

Roosevelt tried to set the tone by invoking the themes of toughness toward Germany, grudging indulgence toward France, and slight suspicion toward the British. He told Stalin that he had made several bets aboard ship that the Russians would be in Berlin before American forces captured Manila, bets that the Soviet leader assured Roosevelt he would lose since Soviet troops had encountered fierce German resistance along the Oder line. The president then informed Stalin that he was now more "bloodthirsty" than ever toward the Germans and would welcome a renewed Soviet suggestion of the execution of 50,000 German officers. Stalin replied that the Germans had carried out random destruction in the Crimea but had devastated the Ukraine in a calculated and systematic way, thereby proving "that the Germans were savages and seemed to hate with a sadistic hatred the creative work of human beings."[6]

On military matters the two leaders discussed upcoming offensive action against Germany. Roosevelt promised offensives on February 8 and 12, with a major one in March, and Stalin promised to work out arrangements with his staff. Both agreed to provide details on their respective fronts at the first plenary session.

The two leaders also expressed serious reservations about Charles De Gaulle. Roosevelt ridiculed the French general as a pompous, self-avowed Joan of Arc, while Stalin, more cautiously, labeled him "unrealistic" and "uncomplicated." Stalin's objection to De Gaulle's pretensions derived primarily from France's failure to make a contribution, either on the Western Front or in 1940 when they "had not fought at all." He said that despite this fact De Gaulle had indicated his intention to place troops on the Rhine River "in permanency." Roosevelt in turn replied that, if the French were to have a zone in the occupation of Germany, an idea with some merit, it should be given to them solely out of "kindness" by the other allies. Without expressing consent, Molotov and Stalin stressed that that would be the "only reason" to give France a zone.[7]

Apparently to impress the Soviet dictator that he was truly independent of his British ally and ready to act as power broker at the conference, Roosevelt told Stalin that he had some difficulty with Great Britain. The British insisted on having the northwest zone of occupation in Germany, much to the president's annoyance, and, moreover, they wished to build up France as a strong power capable of placing 200,000 troops on their eastern border for a period necessary to build up a powerful British army. Roosevelt made much of his indiscretion in mentioning this point to the Soviet leader, promising that he would not disclose it in front of Churchill.

With this exchange, Roosevelt and Stalin prepared to move to the palace's main ballroom where the first plenary session was set to convene at 5:00 P.M. Here representatives of the United States, Great Britain, and the Soviet Union gathered at a round table in a rectangular-shaped 30-by-50-foot room, warmed by a conical fireplace, to begin discussions that would determine the fate of the world for many years to come.

Military matters received considerable attention at Yalta. Stalin asked that a discussion of the military situation take place during the first sessions of the conference, a request that his Western allies warmly endorsed. During that meeting, and in subsequent talks between the military staffs and the heads of state, several issues were addressed: the coordination of offensives on the Eastern and Western fronts in Europe; ways to prevent the transfer of German troops from one front to the other; estimates of enemy strength and ability to fight; comparative Allied strength on land and in the air; and, finally, between the United States and the Soviets, Russian entry into the Pacific war.

These talks were unexceptional and did not generate any controversy comparable to that emanating from the political discussions; therefore, it is not necessary to recount them here in any detail. One area of great Soviet concern was that the Allies not let Germany transfer divisions from the Italian front to the east. Churchill promised, seconded by General Marshall in his report, that the Allies would do all they could to pin the Germans down in Italy, although both noted that it would not be possible to prevent some transfers. On their part, the Western allies wanted assurances that the Soviets would not permit, during the spring offensive on the Western Front, transfer of German troops to the West. This was a matter of concern because military leaders assumed that thawing and muddy conditions in March and April would slow the Soviets down in the east. Unless Russian forces pushed on aggressively, pressure on German forces would lessen.

Another issue of concern to Western military people, and to Roosevelt and Churchill, was the arrangement of liaison between the frontline commanders of the Allied armies. This seemed critical as the two fronts converged, and the possibility of accidental clashes of friendly forces increased. However, since Soviet direction of the war was centralized in Moscow and all decisions were channeled through Stalin, Soviet Chief of Staff General Alexei Antonov would and could not address this question, nor did Stalin provide an answer, except to suggest that the Allies establish a bomb line as a kind of divider among their forces. This the Western allies rejected as constituting an unnecessary restriction on air action. It simply was not possible to reach an agreement on liaison because Stalin would not give his field commanders sufficient latitude to make the necessary decisions.

On the matter of Soviet entry into the war against Japan, an issue discussed at Tehran, and then in 1944 at meetings in Moscow, Soviet and American military staffs carried on talks that were also constrained by the inability of General Antonov and his colleagues to deal with strategy, tactics, or to supply questions without constant reference to Stalin. These are issues more appropriately treated in the chapter on the Far East and are reviewed there.

Each of the three Allied leaders brought to the conference his own peculiar blend of assets and weaknesses. Each had his own world view, and each had major objectives that he hoped to achieve in the postwar era.

Of the three, Roosevelt probably had the greatest strengths and the least coherent conception of how to utilize them. In 1945 he was indisputedly leader of the strongest nation in the world, perhaps the strongest since the days of the Roman Empire. During the war the United States developed a productive capability unsurpassed in history, one responsible for feeding, clothing, and transporting an army of its own of 15 million men and women, while simultaneously supplying its British, Soviet, and Chinese allies. American industrial plants produced 376,000 trucks, 14,700 airplanes, 7,000 tanks, 52,000 jeeps, 11,000 freight cars, and 15,000,000 pairs of army boots for the Russians alone. The United States suffered no bombing of its cities, no forced displacing of its civilian population, no hardship that remotely compared to what the British or Soviets experienced. It also developed enormous military power: an efficient, well-trained, well-equipped army and navy, the latter of which had transformed the Pacific Ocean into an American lake; it was on the verge of perfecting the atomic bomb; and it had 4.5 million forces in Europe.

More than Stalin, at least as much as Churchill, and certainly more than any other American president of the twentieth century, Roosevelt was cosmopolitan in his experience and outlook. Beginning as a youth and continuing until adulthood, he traveled annually to England, France, and Germany, trips that brought him in contact with the governing classes and social elites in each of those countries. At Hyde Park his family received the *Illustrated London News* and other foreign publications, thereby making information about international culture available to Roosevelt even when he was not traveling. He had extensive instruction in foreign language, both at home and in his formal schooling.

His tenure as assistant secretary of the navy during the Wilson administration tended to reinforce his international outlook.[8]

Elected four times to the presidency, Roosevelt demonstrated exceptional leadership qualities in giving the American people hope and sustenance, not to say reform during the Great Depression; in leading them toward victory in a great war; and in inspiring sacrifice, commitment, and unity in times of adversity. He was a master speaker, possibly the best among all presidents in American history; he unquestionably used the radio medium better than any of his political contemporaries. His critics notwithstanding, his domestic and foreign programs had the support and endorsement of the vast majority of the American people.

Roosevelt was also jaunty, self-possessed, confident, cheerful, and capable of inspiring trust and affection. What he lacked in intellect he made up for in temperament. He was not good at abstractions, nor did he involve himself much with philosophical questioning, but he generally understood how to get things done and could absorb information without giving the appearance of listening. He had what one scholar has called effective intelligence.

Despite his many assets, however, Roosevelt was in some ways grossly ill prepared to join his allies in organizing the peace. He held no well-defined or sophisticated world view, although he believed that the United States should repudiate its isolationist tradition and play a more active global role. Furthermore, he thought that a by-product of greater involvement should be a brand of internationalism, which he gave a quasi-Wilsonian, quasi-Lodgeian definition. If World War II seemed to vindicate Woodrow Wilson, it was largely because Roosevelt helped keep the idea alive that American participation in the League of Nations would have prevented war. Roosevelt saw himself as a realistic Wilsonian, as one who would lead the nation forward into an international organization by avoiding Wilson's mistakes. Wilson had been too idealistic, but Roosevelt's conception of internationalism seems strikingly nationalistic and paternalistic, not far from that advocated by Henry Cabot Lodge after World War I. In rejecting Wilson's League of Nations, Lodge had suggested that an organization of the Allies would work just fine to keep the peace; the most efficient league was the "existing league of allies."[9] Roosevelt thought that the British, Soviets, Americans, and Chinese—the "Four Policemen"—should dominate the new organization, with the United States playing the role of moral leadership.

In addition, Roosevelt believed that, because the USSR would play a powerful role in postwar European affairs, Soviet-American cooperation would be essential to world peace. Nothing should be allowed to interfere with good relations with the Russians. Moreover, he hoped to achieve an end to colonialism, although his plans for actually doing so were hopelessly vague and ill defined.

Essentially Roosevelt's Weltanschauung was a stew comprised of lessons from his childhood, views he had picked up at Harvard, faith in conventional Christianity, and a belief in progressive democracy, a mixture spiced generously by political expediency. To Roosevelt the Axis powers represented the truly reactionary forces in the world, while the British, as represented by Churchill, were simply old-fashioned in their views. The Russians were crude and disagreeable but manageable, much like American political bosses. The Axis had to be defeated, the British changed, and the Soviets accommodated. Once he had accomplished these goals and implemented the United Nations, international relations would function harmoniously. Unfortunately, the president only vaguely knew what he wanted for Poland, the liberated countries of Eastern Europe, Germany, and China.

That Roosevelt's physical condition had some effect on his mental capacity at Yalta seems obvious. His health had been declining since 1939, and by the time he reached age sixty his heart was dangerously enlarged. His arteries had hardened like those of a man thirty years his senior. During the final year of the war he slept twelve to fourteen hours per day. Sometimes, as at Quebec in September 1944, he dropped off in the middle of important conversations. By January 1945 he looked terrible and could hardly sign his name. He could not concentrate on lengthy documents, much less engage in strenuous bargaining. Howard Bruenn, a young cardiologist at the Bethesda Naval Hospital who was brought to the White House to monitor Roosevelt's condition, made the correct diagnosis: hypertension, hypertensive heart disease, and cardiac failure. Large doses of digitalis could delay his death but not for long.[10]

Although representing a nation debilitated by nearly six years of war, Churchill brought strong assets to Yalta. Not least of these was the moral strength that he commanded as prime minister of the country that had been engaged in the war the longest and for a while was the lone opponent of Hitler's tyranny. He also brought a healthy skepticism of Bolshevism and of the prospects for effective, long-range cooperation from the Soviets. From his earliest knowledge of them, he saw the Bolsheviks as enemies of the liberties he believed in, and nothing that happened in the interwar period had changed his thinking. As a leading proponent of parliamentary democracy, he scorned the suppression of free speech, the elimination of opposition figures, and the purging of those individuals not subscribing to the one true faith. His willingness to forge an alliance with the Soviets derived solely from his sense of expediency in confronting Hitler and from his belief that he might save democracy by joining one of its enemies in war against another.[11]

Churchill's world view arose from his concern that a single power, regardless of its ideology, might dominate the European continent. He worried throughout the war that the Soviet Union would gain a foothold in Western Europe upon the defeat of Germany, and he developed a military strategy to invade the soft underbelly of the Continent in the hope of interposing British-American forces between the Soviets and the center of German power. But he would have worried about any potentially dominating nation. As he wrote in 1936, "British policy for four hundred years has been to oppose the strongest power in Europe by weaving together a combination of other countries strong enough to face the bully. Sometimes it is Spain, sometimes the French empire, sometimes Germany."[12] Sometimes, he would have added after World War II, it is the Soviet Union.

This is not to argue that Churchill refused to deal with the Soviets. They had assets too numerous to ignore and, given their role in the defeat of Hitler, would require some concessions in Eastern Europe. He believed essentially in a British-American peace that would keep the rest of the world, including the Soviets, at bay. He envisioned a world order in which Great Britain and the United States would proselytize the values of Western civilization, and a world order with relatively little dependence on the United Nations.

Churchill possessed outstanding personal qualities as well. A man of great courage, it often appeared to his associates that he seemed to flaunt danger during the war, needlessly risking his life. Stories abound of his refusal to take to his bomb shelter in the face of *Luftwaffe* attacks on London, of his inspection of damage immediately after these raids, of his daring flights from one military rendezvous to another, and of his defying German submarine assault while at sea. Throughout his early life he recklessly exposed himself to danger in battle, either military or political; certainly he was no shrinking violet in parliamentary debate. One can only speculate about the reasons for his behavior. He may have sought to compensate for his endomorphic body, with its puffy, feminine skin; protuberant, tumescent stomach; and weak, puny muscles. As a youth he suffered untold injuries from aggressive behavior for which his body was unprepared. Like Theodore Roosevelt, himself a nearsighted, asthmatic youth, Churchill may have developed romantic attachments to war because of his personal physical inadequacies.[13]

Indomitably courageous, the inspirational quality of the prime minister's leadership, especially his ability to use the language, stood unequaled among his contemporaries. His phrases excited a generation of his countrymen: "I have nothing to offer but blood, toil, tears, and sweat." "We shall fight in France, we shall fight on the seas and oceans, we shall fight with growing confidence and growing strength in the air, we shall defend our island, whatever the cost may be." "Behind us," he said, "gather a group of shattered states and bludgeoned races: the Czechs, the Poles, the Danes, the Norwegians, the Belgians, the Dutch— upon all of whom a long night of barbarism will descend, unbroken by a star of hope, unless we conquer, as conquer we must, as conquer we shall." As one who worked six to eight hours on every forty-minute speech, including his ostensibly impromptu orations, he exercised great care in his choice of words, which he selected partly for their euphonic quality. His comments were pungent and crisp, and words like austere, somber, and squalid were his favorites.[14]

Concern for detail and an ability to remember it are traits manifested by many outstanding statesmen. In some respects a poor student and a failure at the classics, Churchill had a photographic memory, one capable of reciting lengthy passages from books and articles. He once recited word for word an entire chapter from Edward Gibbon's *The History of the Decline and Fall of the Roman Empire*. On other occasions he quoted poems he had learned as a schoolboy, or essays he had read as a young man.

What he possessed in learning and eloquence he lacked in patience. If boredom is the handmaiden of genius, Churchill epitomized genius. Having committed himself on an issue and familiarized himself with it fully, he would tire of it and move on to something else. He would draft and redraft his speeches, or his messages to Roosevelt and Stalin, or his statements at diplomatic conferences, making his comments inclusive and definitive. He would be terribly impressed with his own performance, and then become bored, refuse to hear responses, and, having expended himself, often fail to participate in further discussion. A better negotiator at Yalta than Roosevelt, he was still surprisingly ill prepared. While voluble and emotional, at the same time he was insufficiently persistent.

Churchill also suffered bouts of extreme depression which tended to immobilize him. Many men of great prominence, whose aggressive behavior allows them to perform brilliantly toward opponents, turn their hostility inward once a foe is vanquished or an issue resolved. For Churchill the result was the "Black Dog," as he described his periodic despondency. General Sir Edmund Ironside, chief of the Imperial General Staff, said of him: "He is a curious creature of ups and downs. Very difficult to deal with when in his downs." General Sir Hastings L. Ismay, his military assistant, wrote that "he is either on the crest of a wave, or in the trough; either highly laudatory or bitterly condemnatory; either in an angelic temper, or a hell of a rage: when he isn't fast asleep he's a volcano. There are no half-measures in his makeup. He is a child of nature with moods as variable as an April day." Although Churchill tried to combat these depressed moods, the onset of which he always recognized clearly, by avoiding hospitals, unpleasant situations, and dreary company, he had only limited success.[15]

A man of massive ego, Churchill's desire to hold a summit conference with his allies derived from his conviction that his presence was required at any twentieth-century Congress of Vienna. "Of course I am an egotist," he said to Clement Attlee. "Where do you get if you aren't?" He had the egotist's concept of leadership: it was his responsibility to govern the British masses, whom he never really understood nor cared much about, just as it was Great Britain's responsibility to continue governing its colonial dependencies. At no time during the Yalta Conference did Churchill respond with such asperity as when he thought President Roosevelt, in introducing the UN trusteeship plan, was issuing a challenge to the British Empire, to which display of temper Stalin reacted with knee-slapping glee.

Unlike his Western allies, Stalin was not an orator or leader in the democratic sense but a reincarnated Ivan the Terrible, a tyrannical autocrat and internal hegemonist who sought external hegemony as well. He saw the end of the struggle against Germany as an opportunity to begin, as one historian puts it, "the externalizing of the Stalinization process" as a chance to guarantee the total security of the Soviet state.[16]

Stalin's style was that of a recluse. He remained secluded from the Russian people, accessible behind the Kremlin walls only to a few of his close subordinates. His Russian suffered from a Caucasian accent, and his speech was slow, methodical, and uninspiring. He did not use the radio to harangue his subjects, choosing instead to address groups of high-level party and governmental functionaries who implemented his policies unquestioningly.

Short and squat with a narrow torso and long arms, the left one of which hung stiffly at his side, Stalin had an ungainly appearance. In his youth he had a thick, attractive crop of hair, but as he aged it thinned, eventually becoming gray and sparse as did the hair in his mustache. As befitting one who did not exercise and regularly availed himself of heavy food and alcoholic beverages, he developed a large paunch. He had a heavily pockmarked complexion, and his coloring otherwise was chalkish. His teeth were irregular, slanted inward, and nearly black. He could appear benign and jovial or quite sinister depending on the issue at hand and one's relationship with him.

The author of a psychological portrait of Stalin suggests that he was the quintessential paranoid personality. A vain, power-hungry man with a keen sense of his own inferiority, he harbored intense jealousies and a mean, vindictive spirit. He never forgot a slight or an insult, often demonstrating Job-like patience in waiting to get even. His greatest pleasure, he once claimed proudly, came in picking the proper moment for revenge, then inserting the knife, turning it, and watching his victim bleed. He combined this vindictiveness with an exquisite sense of timing and ability to dissemble, thus mastering the art of manipulating people and playing them off against one another for his own benefit.[17]

By the 1940s, Stalin had so perfected these talents and constructed his control apparatus that he achieved personal domination to such a complete degree that not even Hitler's power in Germany could rival it. He used the party dictatorship to carry forward industrialization and collectivization as the first step in this process. In the mid- and late 1930s he carried out the next stage, which was domination over the party by executing his old Bolshevik colleagues, executing the executioners, and then the executioners of the executioners.

Stalin's destruction of the Bolshevik party was accompanied by his creation of a sort of personal secretariat, through which he exercised his will within the Central Committee. This command apparatus allowed Stalin and his immediate subordinates to issue orders to leaders of the police system or to other representatives across the country. It allowed him to conduct foreign policy through its foreign section, and during the war it permitted him to maintain personal control of military operations.

Out of Stalin's compulsion for personal control arose the world view that motivated him as the war neared its conclusion. He was not a member of the world of international socialism and never had been. He harbored a deep suspicion and fear that the great mass of the European Socialist community would outbid him for support. For this reason he lived in mortal terror of spontaneous revolutionary activity by Communist parties not dependent on the Soviet Union. Only if he could maintain tight disciplinary control did he favor the success of foreign Communist parties. Otherwise, Communist encirclement was as dangerous to him personally as capitalist encirclement, a danger about which he worried and assiduously reminded his countrymen, whether or not it happened to be real. It sometimes was, although he usually took pains to exaggerate. Most of all what Stalin desired in the bourgeois world was what he wanted from the foreign Communist world—weakness.[18]

His immediate objectives in 1945 were multifold. In the east, Stalin hoped to achieve domination in Mongolia, Sinkiang, and Manchuria, areas bordering the Soviet Union. He also wanted control of the Kuril Islands and all of Sakhalin to protect the naval approaches to his empire in Northeast Asia. Beyond that he hoped to dominate Korea and guarantee that Japan was weakened and rendered ineffectual as a military force. In China he wanted a Communist victory but a dependable and malleable client as well. In Europe he wished to emulate the czars. During the bleakest period of the war, Stalin laid claim to a sphere of influence in Eastern Europe, which included Poland with its eastern boundary moved substantially westward. Finally, he desired heavy reparations from Germany, which he expected to join his allies in demilitarizing and controlling.

His greatest strength at Yalta lay in the Russian contribution to the war effort and the positioning of Soviet forces. Most of the major battles on the Eastern Front dwarfed those in the west, and Stalin's troops killed far more Germans than did the Western allies. His armies, moreover, occupied Poland and other important points in Eastern Europe.

Stalin's strength, however, was not unalloyed. Four years of war had cost the Soviet Union as many as 20 million lives and millions more displaced. It led to the enormous destruction of homes, collective farms, and industrial plants. The severe weakening of the Soviet superstructure created a massive reconstruction problem. Moreover, while his German and Japanese enemies stood at the edge of destruction and the European imperialist powers had been weakened and impoverished, one capitalist nation—the United States—would emerge from the war with unprecedented power.

Notes

[1]U.S. Department of State, *Foreign Relations of the United States: The Conferences at Malta and Yalta, 1945*, pp. 4–5 (hereafter cited as *Foreign Relations: Yalta*).

[2]Ibid., p. 21.

[3]John Kenneth Galbraith, *A Life in Our Times: Memoirs*, p. 200. Interestingly, Churchill reported that it took him thirty-six hours to travel from London to Moscow, twenty-three hours in flight. Churchill to Roosevelt, October 11, 1944, Franklin D. Roosevelt Papers, Map Room File, Box 7, Folder 2.

[4]Jim Bishop, *FDR's Last Year: April 1944–April 1945*, pp. 236–82. Bishop provides an excellent description of the respective trips and of Yalta itself.

[5]Diane S. Clemens, *Yalta*, p. 118.

[6]*Foreign Relations: Yalta*, p. 571.

[7]Ibid., pp. 572–73.

[8]See Robert Dallek, *Franklin D. Roosevelt and American Foreign Policy, 1932–1945*, pp. 3–4.

[9]William C. Widenor, *Henry Cabot Lodge and the Search for an American Foreign Policy*, pp. 229, 292, 298, 304, 318, 319.

[10]John Lukacs, *1945: Year Zero*, pp. 82–83, 93. James MacGregor Burns, "FDR: The Untold Story of His Last Year," *Saturday Review*, April 11, 1970; Bishop, *FDR's Last Year*. See also Hugh Gregory Gallagher, *FDR's Splendid Deception*, pp. 202–06.

[11]Martin Gilbert, *Did Churchill Have a Political Philosophy?* pp. 74, 80–81.

[12]Ibid., p. 95.

[13]William Manchester, *The Last Lion, Winston Spencer Churchill: Visions of Glory, 1874–1932*, pp. 8–18.

[14]Ibid., pp. 6, 30, 32.

[15]See Hugh L'Etang, *The Pathology of Leadership*, p. 156.

[16]Robert C. Tucker, "A Twentieth-Century Ivan the Terrible," in T. H. Rigby, ed., *Stalin*, p. 161.

[17]See Robert C. Tucker, *Stalin as Revolutionary, 1879–1929: A Study in History and Personality*; George F. Kennan, "Criminality Enthroned," in Rigby, ed., *Stalin*, p. 169.

[18]Kennan, "Criminality Enthroned," p. 172.

II
Germany

That the treatment of Germany would comprise one of the central issues at Yalta is axiomatic. Stalin basically knew what he wished to accomplish, Churchill had a rather clear idea of what he did not want but worried that unambiguous advocacy of the British position would endanger future Anglo-Soviet relations, and Roosevelt remained undecided, or at any rate, not fully coherent in his views.

Roosevelt's incoherence derived in part from his inability and unwillingness to accept the arguments of policymaking groups advising him during 1944, and in part from the failure of these groups to synthesize their views. It is not necessary here to detail the history of inter-Allied discussions on Germany, but since 1943 Roosevelt, Churchill, and Stalin all had agreed that the treatment of their common enemy should be harsh, and that unconditional surrender would be required. At the Moscow Foreign Ministers' Conference of 1943, Molotov had demanded large-scale reparations and, less forcefully, the dismemberment of Germany. The foreign ministers also considered the problem of war crimes and agreed to set up the European Advisory Commission, the purpose of which was to decide enforcement procedures once surrender had been achieved. At the Tehran Conference in November 1943, the three wartime leaders discussed dismemberment, or as Stalin put it, "scattering the German tribes." While all seemed to agree that some form of partition or breakup was required, they came to no firm understanding, although they decided that for occupation purposes Germany would be divided into three zones. Firm decisions on reparations, a point of great concern for the Soviets, also were postponed.

Between the Tehran Conference and the summer of 1944, the United States took part in three sources of planning for postwar Germany. In London, U.S. Ambassador John G. Winant and his assistants, George F. Kennan, Philip Mosely, and E. F. Penrose, participated in deliberations of the European

Advisory Commission, which worked out the occupation zones for Germany. Although President Roosevelt preferred that the American zone be in northwest Germany, the plan that the commission devised and that the United States eventually accepted on May 1, 1944 provided for a division in which the Soviet Union received the eastern sector, the British the northwest, and the United States the southwest. The European Advisory Commission also made provision for the disarming of Germany and the Allied imposition of firm controls in economic, political, and military matters.[1]

In the spring of 1944 the Combined Chiefs of Staff in Washington issued directives to General Dwight D. Eisenhower which called for both harsh and lenient treatment of Germany. Eisenhower and his forces were to carry out a thoroughgoing purge and arrest of Nazis in positions of power. They also were ordered, however, to retain Germany's administrative system, to preserve its industry, and to revive agricultural production in an attempt to make that country as self-supporting as possible. These directives were eventually incorporated in the *Handbook for Military Government of Germany.*

The State Department, meanwhile, began preparing its own plans for postwar Germany. Following the advice of Mosely and Leo Pasvolsky, an economist who served as counselor to the secretary of state, Cordell Hull placed his approval on a moderate program. The State Department plan called for occupation zones but opposed partition and harshness in economic matters. Its statement on economic policy, the handiwork of Pasvolsky and Assistant Secretary of State Dean G. Acheson, recommended Allied control and reduction of German economic power rather than the rapid reintegration of Germany into the world economy. In the key area of reparations, which was to cause so much difficulty later on, the department opposed the confiscation of capital machinery and urged that collections come in kind from current production. This required keeping both agricultural and industrial activity at a fairly high level.[2]

Under the guiding direction of Secretary Henry Morgenthau, Jr., an old friend and neighbor of President Roosevelt, and Harry Dexter White, Morgenthau's chief adviser, the Department of the Treasury quickly challenged the State Department plan. The result was contention, confusion, and conflicting advice to a president who was notoriously reluctant to choose between contending points of view.

The Treasury proposal, which soon became known as the Morgenthau Plan, had its origin during the secretary's trip to Europe in August 1944 for inspection of financial arrangements in occupied France. As Morgenthau, at White's instance, read the State Department's policy of reconciliation and the War Department's handbook, he became convinced that, unless someone took a stand in support of a punitive approach, Germany might soon reemerge to challenge European peace. At a luncheon meeting on August 12 held at Redrice, an elegant country house near Andover in Hampshire which served as Morgenthau's English residence, the secretary and White unveiled several ideas that they had been pondering. Present at the meeting were Ambassador Winant, his adviser Mosely, and several other State and Treasury officials. The ideas envisioned the destruction of Germany's industrial power and the reduction of the country to the status of a tenth-rate pastoral nation, a "barren farm country" as Morgenthau expressed it.[3]

After his return to Washington on August 17, Morgenthau met with President Roosevelt, who always agreed with the last adviser to see him, and led the secretary to believe that he wanted to get tough with both Germany's leaders and its people. Leaving the conference convinced that the president would support a plan such as he and White had outlined in England, Morgenthau then established a special committee within the Treasury to work out the details. In turn, President Roosevelt appointed a cabinet committee composed of Morgenthau, Hull, and Secretary of War Henry L. Stimson to confer about Germany's treatment.

Insistent that Germany be dismembered, demilitarized, and deindustrialized, Morgenthau guided his Treasury Committee toward a report confirming his views. "They have asked for it," he said in reference to the German people, and he planned to give it to them full measure. He recommended total destruction of the Ruhr, proposing that army engineers should go "into every steel mill, in every coal mine, every chemical plant, every synthetic gas business . . . put dynamite in and open the water valves and flood and dynamite." To the suggestion that this would cause enormous hardship, he replied: "Why the hell should I worry about what happens to their people."[4] The plan that emerged from the Treasury Committee, drafted largely by White, faithfully reflected Morgenthau's views. It called for demilitarization, restructure and reeducation of the German society, partition of the country, and total elimination of Germany's war-making capability. It also included a provision for the destruction of the Ruhr. It did not call for large reparations but only for the seizing of German assets outside the country, the use of forced labor, and the transfer of German resources and territory.

On the question of reparations and the Ruhr, Morgenthau came into some conflict with White. The latter, in view of his open admiration for the Soviet Union, not to speak of later allegations strongly supported by circumstantial evidence that he passed secrets to Russia, may have believed that because the Soviets would want huge reparations it would be imprudent to destroy the Ruhr totally. In any event, White had no trouble favoring dismemberment and the imposing of harshness, but he contested his superior over the Ruhr. What would the Allies do with the 18,000,000 Germans who would be put out of work, he asked? Morgenthau replied that an international Tennessee Valley Authority manned by Germans could work on projects around the world.[5]

The secretary of the treasury held a dinner party at his home on September 4, to which he invited White, along with Stimson and John J. McCloy from the War Department, for the purpose of revealing the work of his committee. At this meeting and at a session the following day with other members of the cabinet group on Germany, Stimson attacked the Morgenthau Plan in the most vigorous terms. On the matter of the Ruhr, the core of the Treasury plan, the secretary of war said he could "conceive of endeavoring to meet the misuse which Germany has made of this production by wise systems of control or trusteeship or even transfers of ownership to other nations. But I cannot conceive of turning such a gift of nature into a dust heap."[6]

To Stimson, as well as to many historians, Morgenthau seemed to be allowing his revulsion at Hitler's tyranny to cloud his judgment. Whatever the Treasury secretary's motives, whether based on his hatred of Germans, derived from his Jewish heritage, or on his well-known belief in Jeffersonian agrarianism, his plan appears vindictive and of dubious merit in promoting European stability.

Despite Stimson's protestations, Morgenthau attracted the attention of President Roosevelt, who seemed, at least for a time, to show the plan some favor. Particularly impressed with Treasury arguments against the thesis that Europe as a whole required a strong industrial Germany, and with the suggestion that a weakened Germany would have a salutary effect on Britain's search for markets for its coal and steel after the war was over, the president invited Morgenthau to participate at the Quebec Conference in mid-September. Roosevelt also heartily approved of Morgenthau's proposal to rid Germany of its martial symbols—its military parades and uniforms—although a problem with the latter was that roughly 5 million Germans would have nothing else to wear but their uniforms.

That Morgenthau was able to secure Churchill's approval of the Treasury plan at Quebec is less a tribute to the secretary's persuasive powers than to the ability of U.S. negotiators to use British interest in a new Lend-Lease agreement in achieving a quid pro quo. When Morgenthau first presented his ideas on the evening of September 13, Churchill attacked him in his most vitriolic language, stating that whether he knew it or not the secretary was proposing that "England be chained to a dead body." Churchill, Morgenthau later admitted to Stimson, "was even more angry than you, Harry." The next day, however, the prime minister came around in a surprising about-face, which White, who was also at Quebec, attributed to a deal in which the United States gave Churchill assurances on phase two of Lend-Lease in return for agreement on the Treasury's German plan.[7] Phase two of Lend-Lease was the program under which Great Britain was to receive aid between the defeat of Germany and the end of the war against Japan.

The memorandum that Churchill and Roosevelt signed on September 15, 1944 endorsed the Morgenthau Plan. Among other things the document stated that "the program for eliminating the war-making industries in the Ruhr and Saar is looking forward to converting Germany into a country primarily agricultural and pastoral in its character."[8] British Foreign Minister Anthony Eden, who arrived at Quebec on the day the memorandum was signed, became terribly upset at the prospective economic treatment of Germany and remonstrated with Churchill that "we have a lot of things in the works in London which are quite different."[9] To this Churchill replied by delivering a blistering attack on his foreign minister which put Eden out of sorts for the remainder of the conference.

Indeed the British had other plans in the works for Germany, some of them most interesting for what they foreshadowed in the area of Soviet-Western relations. British policymakers correctly believed that future Anglo-Soviet friction would develop less out of ideological differences, although these were obviously considerable, than out of disagreements over the treatment of postwar Germany. At the time of the second Quebec Conference, British officials were operating on the assumption that the Soviets desired "the most drastic measures to keep Germany in a permanent state of weakness." As part of their objectives, they wished the complete dismemberment of Germany and the use of German labor and goods to restore the economy of the Soviet Union. The final test that the Soviets would apply to their natural suspicions of the West was the attitude taken by the British and Americans regarding Germany. In other words, Soviet-Western cooperation would depend in large measure on Western policy toward Germany.[10]

If this was the official view, it was by no means the only one being bruited about in England. By late summer 1944 the Chiefs of Staff and the War-Foreign Office group known as the Post Hostilities Planners were envisioning the Soviet Union as a potential enemy and were speaking openly of the establishment of a Western European bloc to contain the Soviets. Germany, or a section of it, would be incorporated into this Western group, on the assumption that denying the resources of that country to a hostile power was vital to the security of the British Isles. If the Western bloc were itself to utilize these German resources, it made no sense to follow a proposal as put forward by Secretary Morgenthau.

Out of this plan for a Western European bloc came an interesting and ironic suggestion on dismemberment. The Post Hostilities Planners advanced the argument that such assistance as would be needed to confront a hostile Soviet Union would not likely be derived from a unified Germany. On the other hand, they stated, "we might hope to bring parts of a dismembered Germany into a North Western European Group, thus adding strength to this group and increasing the depth of our defenses."[11] By late summer 1944, British officials were therefore seriously considering dismemberment as a way to retain German resources in the interests of a prospective Western alliance.

A certain degree of dualism still remained a part of British policy until the Yalta Conference; that is, two strains of thought competed for ascendancy within British official circles, and the British position fluctuated in large measure according to what would bring the greatest apparent advantage in relation to the Soviets. One problem in the fall of 1944 was that Soviet delegates to the European Advisory Commission seemed to have moved away from their position on dismemberment taken at Tehran in favor of treating Germany as a single unit. If the Soviets were considering a unitary Germany as an ally against Great Britain, the British could see real advantage in dismemberment.

Churchill himself was probably of two minds on the issue. In his discussions with Stalin in mid-October 1944, he revealed details of the Morgenthau Plan to his Russian host and warmly endorsed the plan. He and Stalin seemed to agree that a harsh peace was necessary, and that some form of dismemberment should be imposed. Reflecting on the minimal difference of opinion between the Soviet leader and himself, Churchill said it was "a pity that when God created the world he had not consulted them."[12] By December his comments seem to have placed him in agreement with Eden in that Draconian deindustrialization and dismemberment would be impractical and counterproductive.

Actually the Quebec memorandum that Churchill signed did not place him irrevocably on the side of dismemberment since it mentioned nothing of how Germany was to be permanently divided or what territory it was to lose. This enabled the prime minister to oppose a commitment on the matter at the Yalta Conference, where, incidentally, the Soviet position seems to have been clarified. Although Roosevelt and Churchill, along with their respective staffs, had discussed the treatment of Germany at some length, actually three issues, in addition to dismemberment, remained unresolved: deindustrialization, reparations, and partition for the purpose of occupation. It is important to keep these items in proper perspective. As post-Quebec events demonstrated, it was possible to envision a basically pastoral Germany that was also partially industrial.

Roosevelt still did not know what he wanted to do about Germany, as several events soon after Quebec led him away from the certainty of Morgenthau's proposal. Knowledge of the Soviets' desire for reparations from current production, combined with Churchill's lukewarm consent to deindustrialization, were a couple of influences on him, as was the political pressure that began to build as the press picked up stories on the possible Carthaginian treatment of Germany. By early October the president acknowledged that Morgenthau had "pulled a boner." By election time, Roosevelt had virtually abandoned the Treasury plan in favor of postponement.

Morgenthau, who at that time held a benevolent view of the Soviet Union, could not hide his dismay, in part because he believed that the deindustrialization and dismemberment of Germany would win friends and influence people in the Kremlin. If Stalin knew that the United States favored harshness, Morgenthau thought, "he would act much better." Accordingly, he had urged Roosevelt to send him to the Soviet Union to explain his plan for the Ruhr to Stalin, in the belief that Ambassador Averell Harriman was less credible than himself. "Harriman can't do this. You ought to send me. I get along very well with the Russians and you can check with Stalin as to whether I do or I don't."[13] What Morgenthau did not know in the fall of 1944 was that the Soviets may have been less enthusiastic about deindustrialization than he believed. Indeed, just before the Yalta Conference a Soviet TASS correspondent confided to him that Germany should have "large-scale industry" but under a system of government control and Allied supervision.[14]

When the Yalta Conference convened, President Roosevelt indicated his desire to focus on only two of the questions relating to Germany: final approval of the zones of occupation, and French participation in the occupation and in the Allied control machinery. Stalin wanted to discuss dismemberment and reparations, with great emphasis on the latter, while Churchill favored the limited agenda put forward by Roosevelt. On February 5 the three leaders addressed these questions directly at the second plenary session of the conference.[15]

The question of French participation in the occupation had arisen during the early fall of 1944 when General Charles De Gaulle began insisting that France, which had been liberated in August and September, be included not only in the occupation but also in all the major Allied decisions on Germany. In January, De Gaulle requested French participation in the forthcoming great-power conference, basing his request on the proposition that otherwise France could not be bound by agreements reached there. President Roosevelt, advised by the State Department, gave his lukewarm support to a zone of occupation but did not want De Gaulle at Yalta. Although he did not favor French involvement at the conference, Churchill strongly endorsed France's position.

At the second plenary session, Churchill told Stalin and Roosevelt of the reasons for his thinking. France, he advised, would be needed as a bulwark against Germany, thus relieving the British of the sole postwar responsibility for containing German power, a necessary condition because the United States would not stay in Europe very long after the war, possibly no longer than two years. A strong French ally in possession of a large army would play a role for Great Britain similar to that which the Poles would play for the Soviet Union.

Stalin was only slightly more impressed with Churchill's reasoning than he had been with that of De Gaulle when the French leader had visited Moscow in December. That France had contributed very little to the winning of the war and had collaborated with the enemy were facts that deliberations of the Big Three could not erase. The Control Commission, Stalin thought, should remain in the hands of those powers who deserved control by virtue of their sacrifices during the war. If France were given the right to participate, many other nations would have an equal claim. To this Churchill responded with a remark that must have stung Stalin deeply. In a pointed reference to the Soviets' pact with Hitler of August 1939, he said that every nation "had had their difficulties at the beginning of the war and had made mistakes."[16]

All three leaders agreed at this session that France should have a zone of occupation carved out of the Western zones, but Roosevelt and Stalin both opposed bringing the French into the Control Commission. Accordingly, they decided, as they did on most substantive and complicated questions at the conference, to assign the matter to the foreign ministers for further study. At the foreign ministers' meeting in Molotov's quarters on February 7, Eden insisted that France would not accept a zone of occupation without membership in the Control Commission, nor should it. To efforts by Molotov and Secretary of State Stettinius to relegate the issue to the European Advisory Commission and thus postpone it, Eden voiced his vigorous objection. The foreign ministers consequently could not agree on a recommendation for the next plenary session.[17]

French participation remained in contention until near the end of the conference and only achieved resolution after President Roosevelt reversed himself and took a strong stand in support of the British. On February 9 the British expressed their desire to have France join in the Declaration on Liberated Europe, a position that the United States endorsed the next day during another foreign ministers' session. Also, on February 10, Harriman conveyed to Stalin that now Roosevelt would associate the United States with the British in respect to the control machinery, since he saw no way to give the French a zone without allowing them a voice in its operation and because he thought it would facilitate France's acceptance of the Declaration on Liberated Europe. That the president and the prime minister had coordinated their strategies now became apparent to Stalin, suggesting to him that it made sense to relent on this relatively unimportant issue. The Soviet leader then hastened to announce his concurrence with Roosevelt's position.[18]

Far more important to Stalin was the question of dismemberment. How much he knew about British-American planning for Germany is unclear, but Molotov told Eden and Stettinius, at a luncheon meeting of the foreign ministers on February 5, that the Soviets believed the Western allies to be "considerably ahead of the Russians . . . on this question," presumably meaning that the Soviets, through Churchill, had received knowledge of the Morgenthau Plan.[19] Certainly the Soviets also had been aware of some of the preliminary plans for dismemberment since, at Tehran, Roosevelt had proposed the division of Germany into five parts, and at the same meeting Churchill had recommended a two-part division, including a separation of Prussia from the southern part of the country. At the Moscow Conference with Stalin in October 1944, the prime minister had reiterated his Tehran recommendation, this time suggesting, in addition, the internationalizing of the Ruhr and Westphalia. At the second Yalta plenary session, Stalin reviewed the tentative proposals and then asked his allies if the time had not come to make a firm decision on dismemberment.[20]

Stalin's remarks in this session foreshadowed a sparring match between himself and Churchill that reflected the behind-the-scenes deliberations on dismemberment. Churchill opposed a quick agreement because Stalin seemed to want it so badly and because he had considered "the actual method and a final decision as to the manner of dismemberment too complicated to be done here in four or five days." The prime minister would agree in "principle" but no more. The matter should be given to the foreign ministers and then perhaps to the European Advisory Commission, or some other suitable machinery, for final determination. Actually, Churchill's willingness even to accept the principle is open to question in view of his resistance to Soviet arguments.[21]

In the absence of hard evidence, it is useful to speculate on how Allied opinion was formed on this issue. If British officials were correct in their assessment during the early fall of 1944 that the Soviets seemed to have moved away from dismemberment, why then did Stalin press the matter so forcefully at Yalta? He may have been dissembling, but, if he was, this hardly seems the proper procedure; the only logical conclusion has to be that he favored the idea. The British, on the other hand, seemed to have dropped any desire for dismemberment by the time of the Yalta meeting. Whether the military tides had anything to do with the respective positions is unclear. President Roosevelt, at one point in the discussions, speculated that the partition of Germany for occupation purposes might determine the future breakup of the country, a thought that surely must have occurred to Stalin. Since Soviet armies already had moved deeply into Germany, the Russian leader may have been thinking of the maximum advantage he could gain if the Allies put their imprimatur on dismemberment. The Western allies, much to Churchill's annoyance, would later withdraw to the zones agreed upon by the European Advisory Commission, but it is questionable whether the Soviets would have done similarly had they moved into Western zones.

Given the military situation at the time of Yalta, Churchill could foresee little prospective advantage to Great Britain in a deal that would sanction dismemberment if the result, as surely seemed likely, was Soviet military occupation of a good part of Germany. It would be considerably easier to dislodge the Soviets from Germany if the Allies agreed to treat the country as one unit rather than as several.

Roosevelt sought to mediate the Allied dispute, with only limited success. He stated his opinion that the decentralization of Germany into five to seven states seemed a good idea and suggested that the foreign ministers develop a plan that they could present within twenty-four hours. Churchill quickly diverted the president, however, by interjecting the words "a plan for the *study* of the question of dismemberment," which was not what Roosevelt had meant at all but to which he assented.[22]

Stalin wanted the surrender terms to call for dismemberment, and he urged that his two Western allies agree to the idea in principle and then designate a special commission to study it. Churchill resisted, a resistance reflected in the foreign ministers' discussion on February 6. Instructed to come up with proposals on including a clause on dismemberment in the surrender terms, the ministers found themselves in disagreement over the wording, with Eden willing to accede only "measures for the dissolution of the German unitary state," and Molotov insisting on stronger language. Stettinius tried to take the middle ground by urging that the ministers agree to a clause stating that the right to dismember Germany was one of the rights the Allies would exercise over that country at war's end.

Having failed to solve the issue of the surrender clause on the 6th, the foreign ministers returned to it the next day, this time deciding to give the problem to their own subordinates. They established a committee, composed of Andrei Vyshinsky, Sir Alexander Cadogan, and H. Freeman Matthews, to study the matter further. The committee finally came up with language that the Big Three accepted on February 11: the Allies would possess "supreme" authority over Germany and, in exercising this authority, would "take such steps, including the complete disarmament, demilitarization and dismemberment of Germany as they deem requisite for future peace and security."[23] On the larger question of a procedure to divide the country, the foreign ministers recommended the creation of a special committee, consisting of U.S. Ambassador Winant, Soviet Ambassador Feodor T. Gusev, and Anthony Eden himself, to meet in London to study the question.

In earlier discussions the Allies had tossed around several rather specific proposals for Germany's division. At Yalta they could agree on nothing except to state vaguely in the surrender terms that they would reserve the right to dismember the country and would establish a committee to study a possible procedure for doing so. Agreement impossible, they passed the matter over to the foreign ministers, who worked out a deliberately ambiguous modus vivendi that ultimately had little meaning. Certainly nothing transpired over this issue suggestive of the need for a summit conference.

The conferees at Yalta also failed to work out a solution on the reparations question. A time-honored view of peacemaking was that the winners should punish the losers, take their property, and divide their territory in a manner designed to preclude future military action by the loser. In the furtherance of their security, the winners should then construct alliance systems aimed at the loser. Stalin was a traditionalist. Having proposed that the Allies agree to the principle of dismemberment, he urged commitment to a specific plan for reparations.

The Soviets brought Ivan Maisky, former ambassador to Great Britain and now deputy commissar of Foreign Affairs, to

the plenary session on February 5 to present their proposal. Carefully prepared, Maisky's presentation recommended two categories of reparations: removal of heavy industry, including
machine tools, plants, and rolling stock over a period of two
years, and annual in-kind payments out of current production
to last ten years. Elaborating on what he intended, he said that
80 percent of German iron and steel, electrical power, and chemical industries would have to be withdrawn in order to restore
the Soviet economy and provide for future European security.
When he said "withdraw," he meant that it would be necessary
to "confiscate" and "carry away physically" these German assets.
He further recommended 100 percent removal of aviation factories, synthetic oil refineries, and other specialized industry that
the Germans could use for military purposes. If roughly 20 percent of its industry remained, Germany could adequately meet
its domestic needs and still fill the requirements of reparations
deliveries in kind over the ten-year period. Those goods that the
Soviets wished included in this latter category he left undeter-
mined. In order to execute the plan and to maintain security,
the Soviet commissar continued, Anglo-Soviet-American control
over the German economy should last even beyond the reparations period, and the Allies should sit on the boards of all
industries that could be used for military purposes.

Maisky went on to indicate the dollar amount that the Soviets
expected to receive. Losses were so enormous from German
aggression that it was impossible to provide adequate compensation, and payments would only begin to cover direct material
destruction. Accordingly, Maisky suggested a formula for establishing priorities, under which the countries that had made the
greatest contributions to the war effort and had suffered the
highest material losses would receive the most reparations. Under
this index the Soviets would expect to receive not less than
$10 billion in withdrawals and yearly in-kind payments. To work
out the details and principles, an Allied reparations commission
would be established.[24]

Churchill objected to the Russian proposal. He acknowledged that the Soviet Union had suffered more than any other
country and deserved reparations, but in a cautionary vein he
said that he did not believe it was possible to extract such large
amounts as the Soviets wanted, and he pointed out the tremendous reparations problems of the post-World War I period. The
prime minister admitted that he was "haunted by the specter of

a starving Germany which would present a serious problem for the Allies." Thinking back to his initial objection to the Morgenthau Plan, he reminded his hosts that, when 80 million people were starving, the Allies could not simply say, as Morgenthau wished to do, "it serves you right." "If you wished a horse to pull a wagon," Churchill pointed out, "you would at least have to give it fodder."[25]

Seeking again to mediate between his two allies, President Roosevelt offered qualified support to the Russian position. The United States would not repeat its mistakes of the 1920s when it financed German reparations through loans. Roosevelt thought Germany should retain enough "industry and work" to keep it from starving, but the Soviets also should get as much as they could in manpower and factories.

Churchill and Stalin both agreed that the time had come to name a reparations commission but differed drastically on its duties and on possible Big Three directives to it. Churchill thought that any differences that emerged regarding the commission should be referred to the government in question, thereby giving each an effective veto over policy. He was also of the opinion that the commission should seriously consider reparations claims of other nations and not just the Big Three. Stalin did not think France deserving since it had suffered less than Belgium, Yugoslavia, or Poland and, to Churchill's argument that France had suffered large-scale destruction at the hands of the Allies, replied that it could hardly expect to receive reparations from the Allies.[26] He further suggested that the foreign ministers work out a directive to the commission. The reparations question, as other difficult matters at Yalta, was thus passed on to subordinate officials.

The foreign ministers, however, were not successful in dealing with the reparations issue. In meetings on February 7 and 9 the three ministers haggled over several points, the most important being the expression of an exact figure. Maisky's presentation on February 7 proved that the Soviets were ready for this discussion, as he explained how they arrived at a figure of $20 billion, of which they would receive half. He said that he and his confreres had estimated the total prewar national wealth of Germany at $125 billion, an amount the war had reduced by 40 percent to a sum of roughly $75 billion. The experience of other industrialized countries suggested that approximately 30 percent of this wealth, or in Germany's case $22 or $23 billion, wás mobile or susceptible to transfer. The Soviets would take $10 billion of the mobile wealth. With the remainder the Germans would have a living standard comparable to that of most Central European countries. Out of the annual German income of $18 to $20 billion, the Soviets would thereafter take $1 billion each year.[27]

Although Secretary of State Stettinius tended to side with the Soviet position, British obstinance made agreement impossible. On February 9 the American secretary proposed, in basic accord with Maisky's plan, that reparations go mainly to those who had suffered the heaviest losses and to those who had contributed most to victory. He also endorsed the Russian plan for transfer of heavy industry and annual payments over a ten-year period. Unlike the British foreign minister, Stettinius had no problem considering the specific figure of $20 billion as the total reparations bill and was willing to recommend a fixed sum to the proposed reparations commission. Eden would not agree to accept a figure, nor would he accept the Russian idea that the purpose of reparations was the "military and economic disarmament of Germany." Since the British obviously did not favor economic disarmament, Eden said that transfers of capital equipment should occur to destroy German war potential. The destruction of Germany economically would create a burden for the Western allies and would conflict with the Soviets' own desire for payments since it would limit the German ability to pay.

The plenary session on February 10 and a dinner that night brought an ambiguous agreement that did little credit to the delegates and provided scant justification for the trek to Yalta. At this session, both Roosevelt and Churchill opposed mentioning any figure, with the prime minister using the argument that his War Cabinet forbade him to do so, and with the president claiming that the American people would misunderstand. They "would believe that it involved money," he argued.[28]

Frustrated in the extreme, Stalin grew angry, at one point rising from his chair to announce that, "if the British felt that the Russians should receive no reparations at all, it would be better to say so frankly." After Churchill responded that he hoped the Soviets would secure large reparations, the Soviet leader urged that the Allies agree in principle to reparations, and that the newly formed Reparations Commission take into consideration the views of the Soviet and American delegations that the amount should be $20 billion, with half allocated to the Soviet Union. Knowing that Churchill disapproved, Stalin then suggested that the $10 billion figure could be used as "a basis for discussions" by the commission. Churchill not only objected to the Soviet-American proposal but also opposed any mention, even for discussion purposes, of the $10 billion. Stalin broke the deadlock by stating that the Big Three simply should instruct the commission to determine reparations amounts. Under this scheme, each party would bring its own figures. Churchill agreed, and, when he and Stalin asked Roosevelt for his opinion, the president said: "The answer is simple; Judge Roosevelt approves and the document is accepted."[29]

The matter seemed resolved, but the Russians, during a dinner meeting on February 10, made one last try to achieve their objective. Stalin told Churchill, in what must have caused some amusement among his own delegation, that he feared going home and telling the Soviet people that they would not receive any reparations because of British opposition. Churchill stated that the contrary was true, and the dinner continued on a very cordial note. At one point Stalin, who expressed warm support for the prime minister in his political situation, indicated that "experience had shown one party was of great convenience to a leader of a state."[30]

When the foreign ministers worked out a protocol of proceedings on February 11, they included a section on reparations that received their chiefs' support, a provision that Roosevelt, Churchill, and Stalin had discussed at the dinner the evening before. The protocol stated that Germany would be required to pay reparations in kind in the first instance to those who had borne the main burden of war, suffered the heaviest losses, and had helped organize victory. Reparations would take the form of removal of heavy industry, as the Soviets wished, but for the purpose of "destroying the war potential of Germany," as the British had proposed. There would be annual deliveries for a fixed period, and German labor would be available for Soviet use. The Reparations Commission, composed of the Big Three representatives, would convene in Moscow. On the all-important matter of fixing the total sum that Germany would pay, the Allied leaders agreed that the Soviet and American delegations would submit a proposal to the Reparations Commission, requesting that it consider for discussion the sum of $20 billion, of which the Soviets would receive 50 percent. The British, while agreeing that the proposal could go forward, still would accept no specific figures prior to consideration of the question by the commission.[31]

Apart from the issue of boundaries, which will be treated in the chapter on Poland, the only other German item of consequence discussed at Yalta was that of war criminals. At the Tehran Conference, Stalin had recommended to Churchill that the Allies round up 50,000 to 100,000 Germans and execute them. Churchill did not see the humor in Roosevelt's response that he favored wiping out only 49,000 members of the commanding staff. There were other frivolous references to the punishment of "criminals" during 1943 and 1944, and there were serious statements on the matter, as in the Moscow Declaration of 1943. Prior to Yalta, however, the Allies had made no firm decisions. Churchill seemed to favor a summary execution of criminals when he first mentioned the topic at the Crimean Conference, but on second thought he suggested "a judicial trial" of those persons whose identities could be established. The Allies then dropped the matter in favor of more pressing issues, on the assumption that the foreign ministers could deal with it later.

Notes

[1]John Morton Blum, *Roosevelt and Morgenthau: (A Revision and Condensation of) From the Morgenthau Diaries*, pp. 560–62.

[2]Ibid., pp. 563–64.

[3]Ibid., p. 587.

[4]Ibid., p. 583.

[5]Ibid., p. 583; David Rees, *Harry Dexter White: A Study in Paradox*, p. 251.

[6]Blum, *Roosevelt and Morgenthau*, pp. 587, 589; U.S. Department of State, *Foreign Relations of the United States: The Conference at Quebec, 1944*, pp. 99–100.

[7]*Foreign Relations: Quebec*, pp. 325–26, Blum, *Roosevelt and Morgenthau*, p. 598.

[8]*Foreign Relations: Quebec*, pp. 466–67.

[9]Blum, *Roosevelt and Morgenthau*, p. 596.

[10]British Foreign Office memorandum, "Probable Post War Tendencies in Soviet Foreign Policy as Affecting British Interests," February 10, 1944, *British Foreign Office: Russia Correspondence, 1941–1945*.

[11]British Foreign Office, document by Sir O. Sargent, August 18, 1944, ibid.

[12]Churchill, quoted in Warren F. Kimball, *Swords or Ploughshares? The Morgenthau Plan for Defeated Nazi Germany, 1943–1946*, p. 48.

[13]*Foreign Relations: Quebec*, p. 371. While Morgenthau maneuvered to go to the Soviet Union, Harry Hopkins confided to the secretary of the treasury that he would like to go to Germany after the war as "strong man" to run the country, especially the economy. He would be bored, he said, with any job in Washington. Morgenthau Papers, September 4, 1944, Franklin D. Roosevelt Library.

[14]Blum, *Roosevelt and Morgenthau*, p. 611.

[15]*Foreign Relations: Yalta*, pp. 611–12.

[16]Ibid., pp. 617–18.

[17]See Diane S. Clemens, *Yalta*, p. 157.

[18]Ibid.

[19]*Foreign Relations: Yalta*, p. 609.

[20]Ibid., p. 612.

[21]Ibid.

[22]Ibid., pp. 626–27 (emphasis in original).

[23]Ibid., pp. 655–60, 699–709, 936, 978; John L. Snell, ed., *The Meaning of Yalta: Big Three Diplomacy and the New Balance of Power*, p. 56.

[24]*Foreign Relations: Yalta*, pp. 620–21, 631.

[25]Ibid., pp. 621, 632.

[26]Ibid., pp. 621–23, 625.

[27]Ibid., pp. 702–03.

[28]Ibid., pp. 901–03.

[29]Ibid.; Edward R. Stettinius, Jr., *Roosevelt and the Russians: The Yalta Conference*, p. 266.

[30]*Foreign Relations: Yalta*, pp. 921–23.

[31]Ibid., p. 979.

III
Poland

Poland, like the Balkans, may be aptly defined as an area of the world that has produced more history than could be consumed locally. So close to the Soviet Union, so far from the West, and possessing no natural boundaries, Poland has experienced 250 years of partition, occupation, and external manipulation. Its emergence as an independent nation after World War I, owing to Woodrow Wilson's Fourteen Points and the Western desire to contain Bolshevism, imbued its people with a heady sense of nationalism that German and Soviet atrocities during World War II could not destroy. That the extent of its borders and the composition of its government would emerge as the most controversial issues at Yalta is hardly surprising. Poland represented a moral and political interest to the Western allies and a security interest to the Soviet Union.

Russo-Polish relations have been strained throughout the twentieth century. At the Versailles Conference, Allied officials, after awarding Poland a corridor to the sea and restoring its traditional territory, arbitrarily established a commission to define the Soviet-Polish border. Out of the efforts of this commission came the Curzon line, so named because of the work of the British foreign secretary, Lord George Curzon. The Curzon line was not satisfactory to either the Poles or the Russians, but the Poles were especially disturbed by the boundary because, in spite of the predominance of Ukrainians and Byelorussians to its east, it permitted a number of their brothers to remain outside of Polish territory. Consequently, Poland used the occasion of the civil war period following the Bolshevik Revolution to invade the Ukraine and move the boundary eastward. After some military successes, Polish forces were pushed back to Warsaw by Soviet armies, whereupon the British and French came to Poland's rescue, a gesture that allowed the country to reverse its losses and ultimately regain territory east of the Curzon line. The Treaty of Riga in March 1921 placed the Russo-Polish frontier 150 miles to the east of the Curzon boundary, to the great and lasting annoyance of the Soviet Union.

Whether Poland had a good claim to the territory given it by the Treaty of Riga is a matter of perspective, but the fact remains that the Poles did not comprise a majority in the region. Certainly the Soviets had a legitimate argument that on ethnographic grounds the boundary was improperly drawn. The Soviets, however, were not in a position to revise it through the 1920s and 1930s. Only after the Munich Conference, and with the events of the spring and summer of 1939, were they permitted to establish a new arrangement.

In an attempt to forge an alliance against Hitler's Germany, Great Britain and France in 1939 began negotiations with the Soviet Union. Although Stalin in an immediate sense saw the British and French as less predatory capitalists than the Germans, he also opened discussions simultaneously with Hitler to secure Soviet interests in Eastern Europe. The negotiations with Britain and France did not work out, primarily because Stalin insisted on, as a condition of entering an alliance, the right to station Soviet troops in Poland, a right that the Poles would not permit because of their long-standing and legitimate suspicion of their larger neighbor.

The result of the simultaneous Soviet discussions with Germany was the Nazi-Soviet Pact of August 23, 1939. In return for Soviet "friendship" and neutrality, Hitler granted the Soviet Union predominant positions in Bessarabia, Latvia, and Estonia, as well as the right to share in a new partition of Poland. The partition began on September 1, when German panzer forces invaded Poland, and was completed when Soviet troops occupied the eastern section of the country less than three weeks later. That the Nazi occupation of Poland provided the occasion for British and French declarations of war on Germany on September 3 gave the country special significance at British deliberations throughout the war.

Hitler was not entirely satisfied with the initial partition arrangement, desiring additional territory east of the Vistula River. Accordingly, on September 28 the Soviets and Germans concluded a further agreement in which the Soviet Union received predominance in Lithuania in return for a German move eastward, a division that resulted in the boundary being drawn roughly along the Curzon line. To legitimize their control in the territory thus acquired, which contained over 10 million people, who since 1919 had been inhabitants of Poland, the Soviets conducted elections, thereby demonstrating the eagerness of these people for Soviet rule.

Both the Nazis and the Soviets dealt harshly with the Poles. The facts about German atrocities against Jews and other Polish citizens are generally well known, but the Soviets likewise herded thousands of their new subjects into concentration camps. With the beginning of the occupation, the Polish government fled to Romania, which itself soon came under German domination, then on to France, and finally to Great Britain. From Britain the government in exile sent military units into action in Italy and coordinated a resistance effort against the Germans within Poland.

The Polish government in exile assumed that the German invasion of the Soviet Union would bring the British and Soviets together and would allow the Poles to write an agreement with the Soviet Union, thus guaranteeing their pre-1939 frontier. After difficult negotiations with Stalin, who remained adamant about regaining most of the territory in Eastern Europe acquired after August 1939, the British signed a treaty with the Russians in the spring of 1942. Meanwhile, the Polish exile government under Premier Wladyslaw Sikorski made a pact in July 1941 with the Soviets which stated that the Russo-German partition had "lost its validity," but it remained sufficiently vague to permit the Russians the thought that something close to the Curzon line would be obtained after the war. In spite of the Atlantic Charter provisions against "territorial aggrandizement," the Soviets did not change their views.

Had Polish leaders been more perspicacious in the late fall of 1941 and less hostile toward the Soviets, they might have turned Soviet disadvantage to their own gain. In talks with Stalin in December, Sikorski extracted a verbal statement from him that the Soviets did not desire that the industrial city of Lwów become a part of the Soviet Union after the war and would permit a slight revision of the frontier east of the Curzon line. If Sikorski could have incorporated this in a general Soviet-Polish agreement, the Poles obviously would have gained an advantage at war's end. Whether Stalin would have committed his proposal to writing is debatable; whether the Poles in exile would have accepted it is not. They believed that a Poland with prewar frontiers was desirable and obtainable and would not approve anything short of that goal.

During the first three years of the war, the eastern boundary remained the central issue in Allied discussions on Poland. With the backing of the United States and the Polish government in London, Foreign Secretary Anthony Eden concluded Britain's treaty with the Soviets in May 1942 without making any commitment to a specific boundary. Fearful that unless the Allies and Polish leaders resolved this issue they would begin quarreling, which would undermine the war effort, President Roosevelt and Prime Minister Churchill in early 1943 expressed a desire for a deal in which the Soviets would receive the Curzon line boundary, or a slight eastward alteration of it, in return for a Soviet guarantee of the postwar political independence of Poland. Sikorski and his cabinet would not agree, much to the annoyance of Churchill, who remained convinced until his death that Polish exile officials had missed an important opportunity.

Events soon gave the Soviets greater bargaining power and allowed them to develop a stronger position on the Russo-Polish boundary and on the political composition of Poland as well. The Soviet victory at Stalingrad gave Stalin greater confidence regarding Eastern Europe as his troops began their advance westward. In March 1943 the Soviets approved the establishment within the USSR of the Union of Polish Patriots, a puppet group dominated by Polish Communists who could be expected to act as a cat's-paw for Soviet positions. The group, for instance, quickly announced its acceptance of the Curzon line and soon drew support from a new pro-Soviet Polish army, also established within the Soviet Union. Stalin then moved toward a complete break with the London Poles, a rupture that finally occurred when the London group raised the issue of Soviet involvement in the Katyn massacre.

The massacre had occurred in 1940 in the Katyn Forest near Smolensk, where Soviet forces had simply executed 10,000 Polish army officers who had been captured during the occupation of eastern Poland. When the Germans found the bodies, they righteously announced that the Soviets had committed the murders and provided abundant evidence to reinforce their claim. The London Poles, who had long fretted about the fate of these officers, gave Stalin the pretext he needed for a break, when in April 1943 they requested an International Red Cross investigation of the incident. Shortly thereafter, the Soviet-sponsored Union of Polish Patriots declared the London Poles unrepresentative of Poland and occupied the Polish embassy in Moscow.

Despite their break in relations with the London Poles, the Soviets pursued a relatively moderate policy during the summer and fall of 1943 because they remained unsure of the response of their Western allies. The British had expressed some degree of annoyance with the Polish exile government for not accepting a boundary settlement, and both Churchill and Eden saw merit in the Soviet position.[1] The United States, however, seemed less predictable. President Roosevelt sometimes implied that Poland was simply a political problem for him, not one with strategic, economic, or ethical dimensions. After the Soviet-London Poles' rupture, he reproached Stalin, reminding him that there were several million Poles in the United States with whom he had to contend, but the president hastened to add that he thought Sikorski had made a mistake by going to the Red Cross.

Roosevelt sent confused signals because he was confused. Apparently willing to accept a measure of Soviet influence in Eastern Europe, he also wanted U.S. access in the region and a settlement there that would accommodate American principles and satisfy U.S. public opinion. Thus he proved unwilling to spell out exactly what Soviet actions he would tolerate or what steps would articulate with American politics.

Meanwhile, American envoys advanced entreaties on Poland's behalf. On a number of occasions during 1942, Ambassador William H. Standley had expressed U.S. concern over the poor state of Polish-Soviet relations, especially over the disagreement on the boundary issue, much to the chagrin of the Soviets who argued that the United States was interfering in an area outside its competence.[2] Moreover, it was largely to generate a spirit of goodwill, which would spill over onto the Polish question, that President Roosevelt sent special emissaries Wendell L. Willkie and Joseph Davies to Moscow. At the Moscow Foreign Ministers' Conference, Secretary of State Cordell Hull sought to promote reconciliation between the Soviets and the exile Poles, an approach that resulted in Molotov's statement in favor of an independent, albeit "friendly" pro-Soviet, Poland. The approach, however, did little to solve the frontier question.

The Tehran Conference of late November and early December 1943 resulted in a general meeting of Allied minds, except for the London Poles, on the Polish boundary. Stalin announced that, if the Soviets received the East Prussian port of Königsberg, they would gladly accept the Curzon line, a commitment that once again appears logical, if not fair, to the historian. President Roosevelt accepted the suggestion, although he went on to say that he hoped that Lwów and the oil fields of Galicia could remain with Poland.[3] Then the president, during an afternoon session on December 1, unburdened himself to Stalin, implying that in fact Poland had little practical meaning to him, unfortunately in the process making his job much more difficult later on at Yalta.

Roosevelt spelled out the political implications of Poland by first stating that he did not wish to run again in 1944 but probably would have to do so if the war was still going on. Should he run, the 6 to 7 million Polish votes in the United States would be important to him, and for that reason he would not take part in any decision on Poland. He said he personally agreed with Stalin, however, that the eastern boundary could be moved west and the western border to the Oder River. His further comments on the Baltic states indicated that to Roosevelt the question was partially one of creating an impression for the U.S. public through some sort of commitment by Stalin to a plebiscite.[4] He could con the American people, who "neither knew nor understood," if Stalin would only cooperate.

Two factors governed Roosevelt's thinking on U.S. public opinion. The one most important to him was the aforementioned concern for his own political fortunes in 1944; Roosevelt, like Richard M. Nixon after him, wanted all of the votes. The other was his belief, shared by many of his advisers, that, unless the Allies satisfied the desire of the Poles and other Eastern Europeans for independent and democratic governments, the American public would react in such a way as to make Allied cooperation impossible on other issues. Secretary of State Edward Stettinius observed that it was difficult to convince people to make a commitment to the concept of a world organization, and "from the standpoint of psychology and public opinion the Polish situation was of great importance at this time to the United States." Assistant Secretary of State Archibald MacLeish spoke of a "wave of disillusionment" that would occur unless arrangements were made for representative regimes in Eastern Europe.[5]

Stalin, who was nobody's fool, immediately saw that he had gotten what he wanted, making his cooperation with the West less necessary. Churchill had agreed to the boundary, to the extent of threatening to repudiate the London Poles if they rejected it. Roosevelt had now given him evidence that Poland simply was not very important to the United States, certainly not worth a quarrel with a major ally. This was an unfortunate message to convey because it grossly oversimplified Roosevelt's aspirations for Poland, which included humane treatment for the long-suffering Poles and acceptance, to some degree, of liberal-democratic values. In any event, the Soviet leader met the president's request for reconciliation with the London Poles with a cynical retort that the latter had connections with the Germans and their agents who were killing partisans. Stalin therefore would have nothing to do with them.[6]

If the West had any remaining hope of achieving a boundary east of the Curzon line, that hope evaporated when Soviet troops on January 4, 1944 crossed over the pre-World War II border. Churchill, who recognized that the London Poles could do much worse, remonstrated with the exile leaders to accept the Curzon line, but to no avail. He at least hoped to be able to secure an independent postwar government of Poland. Churchill also decided in the spring of 1944 that Western interests in Eastern Europe, particularly British strategic interest in Greece, might best be preserved through a sphere-of-influence arrangement between himself and Stalin. Despite the opposition of Secretary Hull, President Roosevelt agreed to a three-month trial of the prime minister's suggestion, which Churchill codified in his meetings with the Soviet leader in October. Under this agreement the Soviets would receive 75 percent predominance in Bulgaria and 90 percent in Romania, while the British would gain 90 percent in Greece. The breakdown of influence would be 50-50 in Yugoslavia.

Meanwhile, during the summer of 1944 the Soviet Union hardened its position. President Roosevelt implored Stanislaw Mikolajczyk, who had become premier of the exile Poles the previous summer upon the accidental death of Sikorski, to try and patch up relations with Stalin, but, before the premier could get to Moscow in July, the Soviets announced the creation of the Polish Committee of National Liberation, which would have jurisdiction in liberated Poland. This new government would be led by the Communist Boleslaw Bierut and left-wing Socialist Eduard Osobka-Morawski.

Stalin then dealt peremptorily with an uprising of Polish resistance forces in Warsaw, to the great horror of Roosevelt and Churchill. On August 1 the non-Communist Home Army, without coordinating its efforts with the Soviets, began an offensive against the Germans, thereby hoping to get the worldwide prestige attending its liberation of the Polish capital and to gain leverage in dealing with the Soviet Union. Although seemingly quixotic, this uprising also appeared necessary to avoid stigmatizing the Home Army as impotent, or even worse, as collaborationist with the Nazis.[7] At first Stalin, who was surprised by the action, seemed to support the uprising, but by mid-August the weakness of the insurgent Poles against the Germans, the inability of Soviet forces across the Vistula to provide military help except at great cost, and political calculations against allowing credit to the non-Communist fighters in Warsaw led the Soviet dictator to insulate the USSR from any involvement.[8]

In the absence of Soviet help or the transport of British and American supplies, which the Soviets adamantly refused to facilitate, the Germans were able to crush the rebels brutally. Indeed, German forces exacted punishment upon the population of Warsaw—man, woman, and child—with a fierceness unprecedented since the Thirty Years' War. When they could find no one to shoot, they blasted away at the corpses. While the British were not entirely pleased with the timing of the revolt, Churchill believed that the plight of the insurgents required an Allied effort on their behalf. Without much success the British tried flying in supplies over the long distance from Italy. Roosevelt then developed a plan to fly missions from France of heavy supply-carrying bombers escorted by fighter planes. This strategy would require landing rights to Russian airfields at Poltava, but the Soviets resolutely refused permission. On August 16, Assistant Commissar for Foreign Affairs Andrei Vyshinsky informed Ambassadors Averell Harriman and Sir Archibald Clark-Kerr in Moscow that "the Soviet Government cannot of course object to English or American aircraft dropping arms in the region of Warsaw, since this is an American or British affair. But they decidedly object to American or British aircraft, after dropping arms in the region of Warsaw, landing on Soviet territory, since the Soviet government does not wish to associate themselves either directly or indirectly with the adventure in Warsaw."[9]

Responding finally to Western appeals, the Soviets changed their tactic in September, agreeing to cooperate in the dropping of supplies from the air, while at the same time blaming the British and exile Poles for the needless carnage in Warsaw. It was too late. On October 2 the remaining insurgents surrendered after sixty-three desperate days. The Polish Home Army was now destroyed.

During the course of the Warsaw uprising, Stalin and Mikolajczyk held tense discussions on the matter of the composition of a unified Polish government. Stalin insisted that the exile Poles be subsumed in a government dominated by his puppet Committee of National Liberation, although he suggested that Mikolajczyk could be premier under the presidency of Bierut. Other conditions that Stalin demanded were the abrogation of the 1935 constitution and recognition of the Curzon line. When Mikolajczyk rejected the Soviet proposals as totally unacceptable and returned to London, Stalin ordered the Committee of National Liberation to constitute itself as the government of Poland, with its capital in Lublin.

A new round of discussions occurred during Churchill's visit to Moscow in early October 1944. In an effort to produce some degree of comity between the London Poles and the Soviets, the British prime minister brought Mikolajczyk, Foreign Minister Tadeusz Romer, and Stanislaw Grabski, speaker of the Polish National Council, to participate with him in the talks, negotiations in which Stalin insisted that representatives of the Lublin group also take part. Aside from Soviet Foreign Minister Molotov's assertion in the presence of Harriman, Churchill, and the London Poles that President Roosevelt had agreed at Tehran to the Curzon line, an assertion that shocked the London group but one that Harriman could not challenge, very little of any significance took place at these meetings.

Relations between the London Poles and the Soviets had been irreparably broken. Soviet ambitions for a malleable and controllable Poland with boundaries favorable to the Soviet Union had caused the break, but so too had the intransigence of the exile government. The London Poles in November refused to endorse Mikolajczyk's tentative agreement to accept the Curzon line, and he resigned. The new government under Socialist Tomasz Arciszewski proved to be even more inflexible than its predecessor, to the considerable annoyance of Churchill and Roosevelt as they prepared for Yalta. Indeed, Stettinius informed Harriman in December that, "in view of the apparent impossibility of the present Polish Cabinet to work out any agreement with the Soviet Government regarding the future of Poland, the Department does not contemplate that relations will be more than 'correct.'"[10]

As Stalin prepared for Yalta, he held confidently to the belief that he could get his way, and that the Western allies would not break with him over Poland. The key was for the Lublin group to pursue moderate policies to prevent Poland from becoming a major "bone of contention" among the Allies. While the British would try to establish a Polish government "dependent on them," Churchill would not be too difficult to handle,[11] nor, Stalin thought, would Roosevelt's views create a problem.

That Roosevelt would acquiesce in Stalin's Polish policies does not mean that during the six weeks prior to Yalta he beheld no serious differences over Poland. The president wanted postponement of the boundary question "until the termination of hostilities," and he hoped that Stalin would refrain from recognizing the Lublin Committee "until we meet."[12] Stalin did not cooperate, informing Roosevelt that "underground agents" of the "emigrant" Poles were killing "soldiers and officers of the Red Army" and were leading "a criminal fight against Soviet troops which are liberating Poland." He saw no reason to postpone recognition. To Roosevelt's response that he believed the Soviets would incur no "serious inconvenience" in waiting one month, Stalin replied that "on December 27 the Presidium of the Supreme Soviet of the U.S.S.R. to an appropriate request of the Poles has already informed them that it intends to recognize the Provisional Government of Poland as soon as it is formed." Stalin was not deterred by Roosevelt's admonition that "up to the present only a small fraction of Poland proper west of the Curzon Line has been liberated from German tyranny, and it is therefore an unquestioned truth that the people of Poland have had no opportunity to express themselves in regard to the Lublin Committee."[13] The Soviet leader could not control the independent-spirited Presidium.

Although President Roosevelt did not, because of his health problems, spend time en route to Yalta studying briefing papers prepared for him by the State Department, he already had formed opinions on the Polish question in close accord with the two main points of these papers. Specifically, on the boundary matter his view and that of his advisers was that, while the eastern boundary could roughly follow the Curzon line, the province of Lwów and the economically important oil fields should remain a part of Poland, which would receive most of East Prussia. However, in the west the only change from the 1939 frontier that the United States should support was inclusion of a small strip of Pomerania. The United States should strenuously object to the Lublin Committee's demand for German territory to include Stettin and Breslau, and thus the transfer of as many as 8 to 10 million Germans. Roosevelt previously had told Stalin he had questions concerning the representative nature of the Lublin government. He shared the State Department's belief that the United States should "take an active part in seeing that in each liberated country liberal democratic groups are given a full opportunity to participate in the activities of the interim regimes."[14]

Condensed, these American interests were twofold: economically, the United States wanted "establishment of a policy of equal opportunity for private American firms to carry on business activities in Poland"; politically, while the United States "would not oppose predominant Soviet influence in the area, neither would it wish American influence to be completely nullified."[15] But, as mentioned earlier, these optimum U.S. objectives could be compromised considerably in a deal that would satisfy American public opinion. Like the Open Door in China, access and opportunity in Poland would be more aspiration than policy.

Proof that Roosevelt was prepared to foreswear the means necessary for implementing U.S. objectives is evidenced by his rejection of the State Department's idea to create an Emergency European High Commission on Liberated Territories. At a pre-conference meeting with his advisers soon after his arrival at Yalta, the president indicated his opinion that this High Commission, the purpose of which was to supervise elections in the liberated countries and to ensure adherence to the principles of the Declaration on Liberated Europe, would be ineffective. Whether it would have been or not is open to question, but it did have potential for placing pressure on the Soviets, and Secretary of State Stettinius thought that Roosevelt had made a serious mistake in rejecting it.[16]

Although Poland was first discussed at the dinner session that same evening of February 4, little of any substance resulted. It is interesting to note that Stalin, in response to Roosevelt's plaintive remark about Polish opinion in the United States, announced that of the 6 to 7 million Poles in America only 7,000 ever voted. Whatever the number, it mattered little to Stalin, who agreed with Deputy Foreign Minister Vyshinsky, whom Dean Acheson later described as one of the world's leading barbarians, that "the American people should learn to obey their leaders."[17]

At the plenary session of February 6, Roosevelt introduced the Polish question and its two main dimensions: the boundary and the composition of Poland's new government. Reiterating his concern about the Poles in the United States, the president said he agreed to the Curzon line but asked for something for Poland, either Lwów, the oil fields, or both so that the Poles could "save face." Roosevelt pleaded with Stalin to make "a gesture in this direction," to which the Soviet leader responded by asking whose face the president wished to save: the Poles in Poland or the "émigré" Poles? On the matter of the Polish government, Roosevelt recommended the creation of an ad interim government that would have majority support. He suggested setting up a small presidential council that would work toward a more permanent arrangement. "What people want," the president said, "is the creation of a government of national unity to settle their internal differences. A government which would represent all five major parties is what is wanted." It also should be "thoroughly friendly to the Soviet Union."[18]

Churchill followed Roosevelt's statement with one of his own in which he noted that, while he favored including Lwów within the Soviet Union, he would heartily endorse a boundary settlement like the one Roosevelt suggested should the Soviets choose to make such a magnanimous gesture. The prime minister's main concern was that Poland would have an independent government: "Never could I be content with any solution that would not leave Poland as a free and independent state." This was not a material interest to the British, who, after all, had gone to war over Poland, but "only one of honor." Churchill wanted a provisional government "pending free elections," one that all three allies could recognize, and one that would have a place for representatives of the London Poles—Mikolajczyk, Grabski, and Romer, all men of good sense in whom the British had confidence.[19]

Stalin called a ten-minute break in the proceedings and then came forward with a statement of his own. He announced that he shared his allies' desire for a strong and powerful Poland, one that could close off the corridor of attack on Russia, a corridor that the Germans had passed through twice in one generation. This, Stalin stressed, was "not only a question of honor but of life and death for the Soviet state." Addressing himself to Churchill's remark that the Allies create a Polish government, Stalin replied sarcastically, and quite hypocritically, that the three leaders could not set up a government at Yalta without Poles: "They all say I am a dictator but I have enough democratic feeling not to set up a Polish government without Poles," although he set up the Lublin regime without consulting more than a handful of them. Despite his desire for unity, he did not see how to get the London and Lublin groups together but suggested that he might be able to bring some of the latter to the Crimean Conference for consultation. In any event, the London, or émigré, Poles had caused nothing but trouble for the Red Army, and their representatives within Poland had killed 212 Russian military men. "When I compare the agents of both governments I find that the Lublin ones are useful and the others the contrary." Nor was Stalin troubled by the undemocratic nature of the Lublin, now Warsaw, regime, for "the Warsaw government has as great a democratic basis in Poland as de Gaulle has in France."[20]

Stalin was unmoved by his allies' appeal to his magnanimity on the boundary question. The Curzon line, he argued, was established not by the Russians but by the British, French, and Americans who drew it on the basis of ethnological data against the will of Lenin. Churchill and Roosevelt, in suggesting that Stalin give up Lwów and the oil fields, were asking him to be "less Russian than Curzon and Clemenceau." "What will the Russians say at Moscow and the Ukrainians?" If Roosevelt could invoke public opinion, so could he. Stalin made it clear he would not budge from the Curzon line. Poland could be compensated for its loss with territory taken from Germany in the West as far as the western Neisse River.[21]

Having made his appeal to Stalin at the plenary session, Roosevelt, on the evening of February 6, sent the Soviet leader a letter that had been drafted for him by presidential adviser Harry Hopkins and State Department officials. The president's missive called Stalin on the latter's offer to bring some of the Lublin-Warsaw Poles to Yalta, specifically requesting that he include Bierut and Osobka-Morawski. To join them and other representatives from London, namely Mikolajczyk, Grabski, and Romer, Roosevelt suggested calling certain religious and educational leaders from inside Poland. Stalin responded to this request the next day by saying that the Soviets had tried to reach the Warsaw leaders by telephone but with no success; it was probably "too late anyway."[22] There is no record indicating whether or not the president believed this fiction, although it is hard to imagine anyone doubting that Stalin could have arranged to have them there within two days if he wished.

In response to Roosevelt's request that the Allied leaders start fresh in setting up a government in Poland, Molotov then presented a package deal for consideration. For boundaries, the

Soviets would insist on having the Curzon line, with slight modification in the east and the western Neisse in the west, but would
permit the addition of certain émigré Polish leaders to the existing Warsaw-Lublin regime, after which the Allies would recognize this regime. Some time later there would be elections to
determine a permanent government.[23]

The Allies then settled down to serious wrangling. Both Roosevelt and Churchill objected strongly to use of the term "émigré"
to refer to the London Poles, arguing that these Polish leaders
had in fact not been driven from their homeland. The Western
allies were no less strenuous in their opposition to the western
Neisse border, as reflected in Churchill's statement about stuffing
"the Polish goose until it dies of German indigestion." Roosevelt
was willing, as he revealed on the morning of February 8, to
allow East Prussia south of Königsberg, upper Silesia, and some
lands east of the Oder to go to Poland, but nothing further. The
president's proposal on the political situation consisted of the
creation of an interim Government of National Unity, composed
of all the Polish factions, that would hold free elections. Once
this was done, a permanent government could be set up, one
that all could recognize. When Churchill spoke up, he agreed
with the Soviet proposals on the eastern boundary and a Poland
bounded in the west by the Oder River. He wanted a truly
representative provisional government and would accept nothing
else. Certainly he would not approve of the Warsaw regime as
it existed.[24]

Would the provisional government of Poland now be merely
an enlargement of the Lublin regime, which is what Stalin and
Molotov wanted, or an entirely new one made up of all factions,
which is what the Western allies desired? Churchill said he would
not repudiate the London Poles or the 150,000 Polish soldiers
fighting in Italy in favor of the unrepresentative Warsaw regime.
Only after a provisional government held free elections would
he drop support for the London group. When Roosevelt and
Churchill "ganged up" on Stalin and pressed him on the issue
of elections, he promised that they could be held in one month,
thus the problem would exist only from the time of liberation
until elections, or thirty days. It was obvious, however, that the
political issue was a long way from being resolved because it was
not clear whether Stalin's promise would be carried out.[25]

Stalin and Molotov had hit upon a way of mollifying the
Western allies. If they promised relatively early elections,

Roosevelt and Churchill could hardly protest vehemently against the Warsaw regime because it would soon be replaced. They might, accordingly, accept it rather than insist on a new government. At the same time, Stalin had no intention of permitting elections that would result in anything but a pro-Soviet regime.

Historians have made much of the elastic nature of the Yalta accords, averring that the deliberate ambiguity written into them allowed the Soviets, after the conference ended, plenty of latitude for self-interested action in Poland, Germany, and northeast Asia. This assessment is not basically incorrect. In Poland, however, it was not a case of elections meaning one thing to Stalin and another to his Western allies. The Soviets knew full well what the Allies intended. During the February 9 session of the foreign ministers, to whose jurisdiction the heads of state had remanded the Polish question, along with all other issues that they could not settle, Secretary of State Stettinius recommended a formula that called for a "reorganization" of the Warsaw regime into one that was "representative" of all democratic forces in the country and abroad. This "Provisional Government of National Unity," which the Big Three would recognize, would hold free elections that would be supervised by the three ambassadors in Poland to guarantee that they were truly free. At this point, Eden argued that he believed that any elections conducted by the Warsaw regime would not be free or "represent the will of the Polish people." Molotov then endorsed a part of Stettinius's proposal but contended quite transparently against allowing the ambassadors to function as official observers since to do so "would undoubtedly be offensive to the Poles as it would indicate that they, the Poles, were under the control of foreign diplomatic representatives."[26] Both Molotov and Stalin, who later backed his foreign minister, knew what they were doing; they knew the difference between free elections and the kind they wished to hold.

At the plenary session on the afternoon of February 9, Molotov not only insisted that the Allied ambassadors be denied the right to observe the elections but also that only those parties which the Soviets defined as "anti-Fascist" be allowed to participate. Both Roosevelt and Churchill urged that the provision regarding the ambassadors should be retained, with the president insisting that the elections be "like Caesar's wife. I did not know her but they said she was pure." Stalin knew her: "They said that about her," he interrupted, "but in fact she had her sins."

Except on the question of the ambassadors as an observer team, the Allied leaders were close to agreement, primarily because Molotov, in presenting the new Soviet proposals, had used the word "reorganized," rather than "enlarged," in stating that Poles from abroad be brought into the government. Although Churchill and Eden still had their doubts, Roosevelt thought only proper drafting stood in the way of agreement. Actually, neither Churchill nor Roosevelt was willing to leave the conference without settlement of some sort, in Churchill's case because of the impression that failure would have on world opinion and in the president's because of concern for the Poles in the United States. This was a debilitating weakness of the Western allies at Yalta and is indeed a problem endemic at all summit conferences: the unwillingness of the participants, certainly those from the democracies, to permit the appearance of failure.

In a long and grueling discussion on the evening of February 9, the foreign ministers, who once again took over the problem, arrived at agreement on several points. They concurred that the Soviet army had created a new situation in Poland; that a provisional government should be set up consisting of the Warsaw regime, on which it would be based, and other Polish leaders from within and without Poland; that Molotov, Harriman, and British Ambassador Clark-Kerr would hold discussions with all Polish leaders later in Moscow to reorganize the Warsaw regime; that this reorganized government would hold free elections; and that the Allied powers would recognize a new government of Poland after elections were held. Once again Molotov objected to the provision for ambassadorial supervision of the electoral process, an objection that he pressed for so vigorously that Roosevelt, who was anxious to return home, agreed the next day to drop the proposal.[27] Churchill and Eden found this concession unsatisfactory and went to Yusupov Palace later on the 10th to reassert the Western position, but the best they could do was a statement from Stalin that recognition of a new government would "entail an exchange of Ambassadors by whose reports the respective governments would be informed about the situation in Poland."[28]

The conferees worked on the wording of the agreement on February 10, and, except for the boundary issue, which still required attention, affirmed their assent to the foreign ministers' proposals of the previous day. Although they approved the eastern frontier, Roosevelt and Churchill still did not like the idea of the western Neisse boundary, and Churchill refused to accept it. However, he agreed that Poland should receive large-scale compensation from Germany and eventually went along with Roosevelt's suggestion that the powers wait and consult the new Government of National Unity before deciding firmly on the western boundary.

Roosevelt, who had a great capacity for dissimulation, conceived a solution in the waning minutes of the plenary session on February 10. Responding to advice from his staff that he might not have the constitutional right to make an agreement on boundaries, the president proposed that the Allied leaders state that the "three heads of government" should "consider" and "feel" rather than agree, but such language would not be binding. What the Big Three finally decided upon, owing largely to Roosevelt, was ingenuously vague and ambiguous: "The three Heads of Government *consider* that the Eastern frontier of Poland should follow the Curzon Line with digressions from it in some regions of five to eight kilometers in favor of Poland." The accord went on to say that Poland would gain German territory in the north and west. It further stated that the Allies "*feel* that the opinion of the new Polish Provisional Government of National Unity should be sought in due course on the extent of these accessions and that the final delimitation of the Western frontier of Poland should thereafter await the Peace Conference."[29]

No formal settlement of the western boundary issue ever occurred. The Soviets eventually transferred a part of the Soviet zone of Germany abutting the Neisse River to Poland, and the Western allies approved the Polish administration of this territory until the signing of the peace treaties. West Germany finally recognized the territory as an integral part of Poland in 1972.[30]

There was nothing here to displease Stalin, nor did he find any provision in the Polish accords as a whole, including the holding of free elections, even slightly offensive. As befitting one who held all the military cards, he had won a smashing victory. The final formula to which the three allies assented stated that "the Provisional Government *which is now functioning in Poland* should therefore be reorganized on a broader democratic basis with the inclusion of democratic leaders from Poland itself and from Poles abroad. The new government should then be called the Polish Provisional Government of National Unity." This government would be "pledged to the holding of free and unfettered elections as soon as possible on the basis of universal suffrage and secret ballot. In these elections all democratic and anti-Nazi parties shall have the right to take part and to put forward candidates."[31]

Stalin's military position gave him a tremendous advantage in negotiating the Polish settlement but so too did the Western approach to the problem. Roosevelt had intimated to the Russian leader, as early as the Tehran meeting, that Poland held significance for him mainly as a political issue. Also, Hopkins later had intimated to Stalin that "Poland per se was not so important as the fact that it had become a symbol of our ability to work out problems with the Soviet Union."[32] Hopkins's main concern was in putting together a package that would satisfy the demands of international theater, hold Polish support in the United States, and not jeopardize the United Nations project by offending the American people.

Churchill, who by all accounts proved to be a tougher negotiator than Roosevelt, confessed at the outset that for Britain the Polish question was primarily one of honor, hardly the position from which to carry on discussions with a determined ally that based its argument on security requirements. More than this, both Roosevelt and Churchill betrayed their all-consuming fear of failure, a sentiment which Stalin quickly turned to his advantage. Every time the discussions reached a stalemate either he or Molotov would imply ominously that perhaps no agreement was possible. "It is frightfully important," Churchill said in referring to the Polish problem, "that this conference separate on a note of agreement. We must struggle precisely for that."[33] To the Western allies an agreement, even a bad one, seemed preferable to none at all.

Given the aforementioned Soviet bargaining chips, could the Allies have secured a better agreement had they been more adept? Most diplomatic historians have accepted the explanations of Churchill and Roosevelt that they did their best for Poland under the circumstances. It is not clear that an ambassadorial observer team could have secured an electoral outcome favorable to the Western position, and it is possible that Western persistence would have resulted simply in a Soviet refusal to agree. However, an observer team might have guaranteed a level of participation by the London Poles and a greater degree of access for the West.

Obviously what Churchill and Roosevelt needed was leverage. George Kennan has argued persuasively that, in the absence

of such leverage, the United States should have separated itself
from the Russian proposals for Poland. It should have accepted
no share of responsibility for them, nor should it have acknowledged the Soviet program for Poland's government or boundaries.[34] Either Poland mattered or it did not. If the United States
and Britain really desired a semi-independent future for the country, they needed more than supplicating words.

Stalin, in sum, came to Yalta with a definite agenda, one
differing substantially from that of Churchill and Roosevelt. To
convince the Soviets to accept a part of the Western agenda—
that is, to make Poland a more humane and less oppressive
society than Stalin envisioned—may well have been impossible,
but one cannot know for sure unless it can be demonstrated that
the Western leaders tried their hardest with the best available
leverage. If Roosevelt and Churchill were going to insist that
Poland mattered at least to some degree, then they must be
faulted for not seeking out every avenue for influencing Soviet
behavior. Ritualistic incantation of democratic principle would
not suffice.

The Western leaders had two cards they failed to play. First,
from the summer of 1944 on, certainly after the Warsaw uprising,
it had become clear that the Soviets intended to challenge the
West over Poland. It is likewise true that after the summer of
1944 favorable circumstances existed to use American assistance
as a tool of diplomacy: Soviet territory had been liberated, there
was no possibility of a new Nazi-Soviet pact, and there was little
chance of a letup in the Soviet offensive.[35] The Western allies,
meanwhile, were advancing in force on Germany. Whether Stalin
valued American aid sufficiently to alter his policy on Poland
drastically is a debatable point, but, as the example of Finland
amply demonstrates, it would have been possible for him to
establish a friendly, pro-Soviet government in Poland without
imposing the kind of regime represented in the Lublin group.
Stalin might have been willing to allow a more liberal Poland if
he had been told that the penalty for not doing so was the cut-
off of Lend-Lease, or he might have believed that he would
require a repressive regime there no matter what in view of his
need to cover up his enormous atrocities. Whatever Stalin's reaction, the important point is that neither Roosevelt nor Churchill
seriously considered such an approach, with the president, as he
put it, always preferring to deal with the Soviet dictator "noblesse

oblige," impervious to the admonitions of former U.S. Ambassador to Moscow William C. Bullitt, among others, that he was dealing not with the "Duke of Norfolk" but a "Caucasian bandit."

The second available card was Allied control of over 2 million Soviet nationals. During the war, Germany took millions of Allied prisoners and interned them in camps far removed from the front lines. Among these were over 5 million Russian and non-Russian nationals, most of whom were taken to Germany or other parts of Europe. Several million of these the Nazis impressed into slave labor details in German factories or fields, where they remained until sickness, starvation, or, if they were lucky, Allied victories brought them release. Hundreds of thousands more were sent to such camps as Auschwitz and Buchenwald, where they suffered unspeakable abuse and died like flies. Of the 10,000 Soviet nationals sent to Auschwitz in October 1941, for instance, only 96 remained alive in January 1945. Over 500,000 donned German uniforms and either fought for the Reich or performed service behind the lines. Some of these men had been forced into German service, some were deserters or defectors with grievances against the Stalinist system who gladly assisted the Nazis, and others were simply opportunists.[36]

In the summer of 1944, when American and British forces advanced eastward toward Germany and the Russians pushed deeper into Eastern Europe, the liberation of prisoners began as German armies were often forced to flee too hastily to make any arrangements regarding their camps. Concern for the health and safety of U.S. prisoners known to be held in Eastern Europe consequently prompted American officials to initiate negotiations with the Soviet Union for the mutual repatriation of prisoners, thereby beginning a lengthy and acrimonious exchange.

In June 1944, General John R. Deane, commander of the U.S. Military Mission to the Soviet Union, contacted the Russian General Staff, which apparently had given no thought to the problem, and cited the camps where Americans were known to be held in Romania and Hungary, requesting that prisoners liberated in the Soviet drive into these two countries be granted proper care. The General Staff responded affirmatively but with no particular plan. Subsequently, because of the prompt action of American forces, the prisoners in Romania were flown out in U.S. aircraft. Then, on August 30, 1944, Deane and Ambassador Harriman formally communicated with the Soviet government. They urged that the two allies agree that, in areas where prison camps were expected to be liberated, a plan be made to repatriate prisoners promptly; that officers from each country be allowed to confer with prisoners to confirm their nationalities and look after them; and that all individuals or small groups found behind their respective lines be quickly identified for nationality.

When by November 6 Russian officials still had not responded to the message, General Deane, now viewing the issue as one of some urgency, requested Chargé d'Affaires Kennan to communicate with Molotov. Kennan then wrote to the Soviet foreign minister, asking him to press for an agreement like the one envisioned in the Deane-Harriman message of August 30. The Russian response, which did not come until November 25, consisted of two parts: a statement that the Soviet Union was prepared "to accept in principle the proposals which Mr. Harriman set forth in his letter of August 30," and a blunt protest accusing the United States of improper conduct in the treatment of Soviet prisoners. The genesis of this charge was the American internment in the United States of some of those Soviet nationals captured while fighting in German uniform, a matter of considerable embarrassment to the Soviets, and the Soviets' attempt to establish a favorable bargaining position for themselves in the subsequent negotiation of a repatriation agreement. Stalin desperately wanted all Soviet nationals returned, whether or not they desired to go back. He was especially concerned about the millions in Western Europe.[37]

In messages of January and early February 1945, the Soviets repeated their protests of alleged U.S. mistreatment of Russian prisoners. The Soviets complained that their prisoners were beaten and forced to work long hours, while German prisoners were not, and that American authorities were denying Soviet officers access to their men. The Soviets were setting up their hand for a diplomatic card game, one in which the stakes would be Allied acceptance of the Warsaw-Lublin regime in Poland.

Meanwhile, U.S. officials began screening out those Russian soldiers captured in German uniforms who, in fact, claimed Soviet citizenship and shipping them to the Soviet Union, forcibly if necessary. In early 1945 they returned more than 3,000 of the Soviet prisoners held in the United States in this manner. Until the war was over, American policymakers believed that they should accept a prisoner's word as to his nationality. The United States, as Acting Secretary of State Joseph C. Grew stated, had "no desire . . . to hold Soviet nationals or to prevent the return to the Soviet Union of individuals who have established claims to Soviet citizenship."

The United States, however, was concerned lest it violate the Geneva Convention of 1929, in which the signatory parties, including Germany, had agreed that the nationality of prisoners was to be determined by their uniforms unless they claimed otherwise. The United States was not simply being legalistic; there were many aliens fighting in the armed forces of the United States, some of whom had fallen captive to the Germans. The Nazis might take reprisals on these men if the United States turned over to the Soviet Union prisoners who claimed to be Germans. In other words, forced repatriation of most of the 4,000 to 10,000 Soviet nationals in the United States, and the millions in Europe, would be unacceptable to the United States, or so it would seem. Secretary of War Henry Stimson and Attorney General Francis Biddle certainly did not budge from this belief. They thought that not only was there danger of German reprisals, but it also would be morally repugnant to force anyone to return against his will to Stalin's jurisdiction. "Let the Russians catch their own Russians," Stimson said.[38]

The objections of certain State and War department personnel apart, those Americans who went to Yalta—and their British counterparts—felt compelled to conclude an agreement that required forced repatriation, in the process essentially succumbing to the dictates of Stalin and his confreres. Reports of stranded Allied ex-prisoners in Eastern Europe alarmed U.S. officials, including General Deane in Moscow and Ambassador John Winant in London, whose son was one of these men. On his part, Foreign Secretary Eden attached less importance to the fate of Soviet refugees than to that of liberated British servicemen who might suffer Soviet reprisals unless the Allies reached agreement as soon as possible. His proposal for a speedy settlement of the issue was almost identical to one put forward by the Russians a short time before. Those men primarily responsible for negotiating the repatriation agreement at Yalta were Ambassador Harriman, Secretary of State Stettinius, and General Deane from the United States; Foreign Secretary Eden and General W. B. Burrows from Great Britain; and Foreign Minister Molotov and General A. A. Gryzlov from the Soviet Union.

The agreement stipulated: 1) that Soviet citizens liberated by the United States or Britain and American or British forces liberated by the Soviet Union would be promptly kept apart from enemy prisoners of war and held in separate camps until they could be handed over to their respective authorities; 2) that the respective military authorities would inform each other about citizens found or liberated and permit repatriation representatives to go immediately to the camps or points of concentration of their citizens, at which point these representatives would take over administration and control of the camps; 3) that facilities be provided for the dispatch and transfer of officers to the camps or concentrations; and 4) that all citizens or prisoners found or liberated would be adequately sheltered, fed, clothed, and cared for until repatriated.[39] Neither President Roosevelt nor Prime Minister Churchill made any effort to apportion the cost of repatriation, although the U.S. negotiators suggested it in a draft proposal, which meant in practice that the Soviets would pay the bill for roughly 60,000 British and American servicemen, while the United States and Great Britain had to cover the cost of millions of Soviet citizens in Western Europe.

Roosevelt himself was as oblivious to the fact that the agreement also meant the forced repatriation of Soviet citizens as he was to the fact that Stalin, who was paranoid that men from this source would be reorganized into a partisan army, would have paid a considerable price to get them back.[40] Moreover, the Western allies did not trouble themselves that the agreement gave the Soviets the virtual right of extraterritoriality behind Western lines in return for nothing but vague promises from Stalin and Molotov of Western access to Soviet-occupied zones.

As events transpired, the Soviets shortly after Yalta proved adept at using the repatriation issue to their advantage. In mid-February, General Deane met three American officers, who not only told of their escape from the Germans and advance eastward into the Soviet Union but also of wandering groups of American ex-prisoners in Poland who needed assistance. At about the same time, the Polish minister in Moscow informed Deane of the existence of approximately 3,000 Americans in Poland, while word of those who had been liberated arrived almost daily. In view of these developments, Deane contacted General K. D. Golubev, deputy administrator of the Russian Repatriation Commission (a man, said Deane, "with the largest body and smallest brain" he had ever met), with a plan to send American contact teams of three to five men close behind the Russian lines in Poland and to fly the wounded or sick out to a hospital at Poltava. The Soviet general listened to the plea and then stated that U.S.

contact teams could be sent only to Odessa and Murmansk, which were extremely long distances from the liberation sites of most prisoners. Finally, after much discussion, Stalin permitted Deane to send a group of men to Lublin but delayed their departure until the end of February and then severely restricted their movement. "Restrictions," General Deane reported, "even ran to a point-blank refusal by the Russian commandant to allow Colonel [C. B.] Kingsbury, the American medical officer, to visit two seriously wounded Americans known to be within a few miles of Lublin."[41]

By early March the matter was so important and the concern so acute that U.S. officials in Moscow called upon President Roosevelt for an appeal to Stalin, an appeal that the president made on March 3. Roosevelt "urgently" requested authorization for ten American aircraft to operate between Poltava and places in Poland where American ex-prisoners might be located. It was especially important to help the sick and wounded. "I regard this request," the president concluded, "to be of the greatest importance not only for humanitarian reasons but also by reason of the intense interest of the American public in the welfare of our ex-prisoners of war and stranded aircraft crews."[42]

Throughout March the American diplomatic and military team in Moscow, as well as Roosevelt, made frequent appeals and protests. All were to no avail; all were parried by one Soviet thrust after another. Stalin's reply to the president's first message stated that "there is no necessity to carry on flights of American planes from Poltava to the territory of Poland on the matters of American prisoners of war" because "on the territory of Poland and in other places liberated by the Red army, there are no groups of American prisoners of war." Ambassador Harriman in Moscow quickly pointed out to Roosevelt the falsity of this statement, informing him that he was "outraged . . . that the Soviet Government has declined to carry out the agreement signed at Yalta."[43] He also pressed the Soviets to allow General Deane to go to Poland, which they at first authorized and then disapproved. The Soviets also informed him they would not permit the U.S. contact team to stay in Lublin beyond mid-March.

These developments further outraged Harriman. He informed the president that he believed very strongly "that we should make an issue of the matter of having our much needed contact officers in Poland which is clearly within our rights under the prisoner of war agreement signed at Yalta."[44] He urged Roosevelt to protest again to Stalin, drafting a note which he indicated should be used as a basis for the message. The president wrote Stalin on March 17: "Frankly, I cannot understand your reluctance to permit American officers and men to assist their own people in this matter. This government has done everything to meet each of your requests."[45] This time Stalin rebuffed Roosevelt with a rude comment that the Soviet army could not be bothered with extra officers among them, and, at any rate, American ex-prisoners were receiving better treatment "than former Soviet prisoners of war in American camps where they have been partially placed together with German prisoners of war and where some of them were subjected to unfair treatment and unlawful inconveniences up to beating."[46]

Harriman's contempt for the latest example of Soviet conduct was unconcealed. To him, Stalin's reply was preposterous. "When the story of the treatment accorded our liberated prisoners by the Russians leaks out," he wrote the president, "I cannot help but feel that there will be great and lasting resentment on the part of the American people." He wanted retaliation of some sort, including the consideration of restricting the movement of Russian contact teams behind American lines, or possibly a cut-back in Lend-Lease aid. The prisoner issue, in which Soviet contempt for basic human values came quickly to the surface, was a most important factor in Harriman's belief that the United States should change the basis on which it dealt with the Soviet Union.[47]

If President Roosevelt, as suggested in his message of March 17 to Stalin, "could not understand" Soviet reluctance to cooperate on the prisoner-of-war issue, many policymakers, including Harriman, soon perceived the reasons. The Russians were relating the prisoner question to the larger issue of the status of Poland, in regard to which they had two primary objectives: to prevent American and British access to Poland until they had established their mission of setting up a friendly puppet government in power, and to achieve recognition of the Polish provisional government.

The three members of the Polish Commission decided upon at Yalta—Molotov, Harriman, and Clark-Kerr—could not agree at their discussion in Moscow on the matter of consultation with prospective new members of the provisional government of Poland. Molotov insisted that only those Poles who favored the Yalta solution should be permitted to discuss reorganization (this excluded most London Poles), while Harriman and Clark-Kerr insisted that certain Polish exile leaders be included. While this disagreement continued, word circulated to Harriman and the British ambassador that the Russians and the Lublin government were arresting, deporting, and executing members of the Polish underground in the process of consolidating their power. While all this was going on, Molotov in late February offered to allow American and British officials to go to Poland to see, as Churchill put it, "what is going on for themselves."[48]

Since Molotov was not given to fits of spontaneity, it seems apparent that Stalin had approved this offer just as he approved, simultaneously, General Deane's proposal to send a team of officers to Lublin to look after U.S. prisoners, albeit on a severely restricted mission. As mentioned, the Soviets on February 26 also authorized a trip by Deane himself, but they soon had second thoughts. It apparently occurred to the Soviet leaders that the visits could be part of a quid pro quo in which they would secure recognition of the Warsaw regime. In any event, on March 1, Molotov seemed less interested in allowing British and American visitors to Poland, and then on March 12 he disapproved Deane's trip. There followed the aforementioned series of negative replies on U.S. proposals for aiding its liberated prisoners of war, and the Russian Foreign Office continued to fling charges regarding American treatment of Soviet prisoners.[49]

The Soviets soon revealed their purpose. When Harriman visited with Molotov on March 14, urging him to allow contact officers access to liberated prisoners, the Soviet foreign minister stated that the Soviet government and the Polish provisional government were fulfilling their obligation under the Yalta agreement, and both the Red Army and the Polish government objected to the presence of American officers in Poland. Harriman reported that when he

> pressed him [Molotov] on what valid objection the Red army could possibly have, he pointed out that we had no agreement with the Polish Provisional Government. In spite of my contention that this was a Soviet responsibility he kept reverting to the above fact. I then directly asked him if he was implying that we should make such an arrangement with the Poles and if so, whether the Red Army would remove its objections. He did not answer this question directly but left me with the impression that he wished me to draw that deduction.

The American ambassador then informed Secretary of State Stettinius that "I feel that the Soviet Government is trying to use our liberated prisoners of war as a club to induce us to give increased prestige to the Provisional Polish Government by dealing with it in this connection."[50] Upon receiving this message from Harriman, the secretary quickly transmitted it to Roosevelt, along with a covering memorandum stating that "it would appear that the Soviet authorities may be endeavoring to use our desire to assist our prisoners as a means of obliging us to deal with the Warsaw Government." The president was deeply irritated by this news and responded with his March 17 message to Stalin.[51]

The British, who had proposed sending a high-level team of observers to Poland on behalf of the Polish Commission, also realized the Soviet purpose of preventing any further contact with liberated prisoners unless they first received recognition of the provisional government. Churchill wrote that "the Soviet Government suspects that the contact officers would, under cover of dealings with prisoners of war, proceed to contact Polish leaders and, in fact, convert themselves into the proposed observation mission."[52]

In April the United States decided it was useless to press for contact teams in Poland, despite the provision for them in the Yalta accord. Thereafter, the Soviets repatriated Americans in their own way and at their own pace, while many suffered—and some died—from lack of food, shelter, or medical care. The Russians, in the meantime, strengthened the provisional government and signed a mutual assistance agreement with it, while the Western allies, after Hopkins's mission to Moscow in late May, concluded a face-saving accord with the Soviets which left control of Poland with the Warsaw government, the composition of which was mainly Communist.

Meanwhile, the Soviets, in what has to be one of the most reprehensible acts in a war not known for its participants' sensitivity to human suffering, had full access to their nationals in the West and oversaw the forced repatriation of millions of them. To Stalin any soldier who fell into enemy hands became a traitor. Moreover, when Soviet nationals, either soldiers or civilians, were repatriated, police met them at the ports of entry and either shipped them off to labor camps in Siberia or central Asia or executed them, a fact confirmed by numerous sources including the accounts of Aleksandr Solzhenitsyn and Svetlana Alliluyeva. Harriman reported on June 11, 1945 that, although repatriation had been under way for months, "embassy knows of only a single instance in which a repatriated prisoner has returned to his home and family in Moscow."[53] Obviously those who had fought in

German uniform could expect summary treatment, but Stalin did not make distinctions; liberated civilian laborers and soldiers held in prison camps were subjected to similar atrocities. As a result, Soviet nationals resisted repatriation, with a great number of them committing suicide rather than returning.

Leaving aside the moral question connected with British-American policy (as Dean Acheson noted, it went "against our traditional policy of political asylum"), one has to address the lack of foresight of the Western allies' failure to seek diplomatic leverage with the Soviets at Yalta from their control of these displaced nationals. That Stalin desperately wanted every single one of them returned without condition was made abundantly clear at every opportunity. His subordinates had a plan ready at Yalta to do just that. *Pravda* published crude, semihysterical attacks on the Western treatment of Soviet prisoners, alleging British-American atrocities. Stalin's well-documented paranoia and his seemingly insane treatment of the millions who were repatriated suggest a frantic concern that his imperialist allies might allow the creation of a military force from these displaced persons for an attack on the Soviet Union. Moreover, the fact that over 500,000 of them already had fought in German uniforms against the Socialist fatherland could not have been reassuring to him.[54]

Only a few officials in the United States—Joseph Grew, Robert Murphy, Alexander Kirk, and Dean Acheson from the State Department; Henry Stimson from the War Department; and Francis Biddle of the Justice Department—had studied the repatriation question, but they had done so in depth and knew what was at stake before the Crimean Conference. Unfortunately for reasons that cannot be explained, neither Roosevelt, Churchill, nor their respective military personnel had done so. The military people wanted immediate repatriation to protect Allied ex-prisoners in Soviet hands and to reduce the number of refugees for which the Allies would have responsibility. Roosevelt had apparently given the matter no thought whatsoever. In his desire to demonstrate Allied unity and secure commitment to the United Nations, he may have overlooked the opportunity to bargain from a position of strength.

The Soviet Union had far more at stake than did the Western allies. The existence of over 2 million of its nationals in the west was potentially damaging to its economy, prestige, and security. The least that Churchill and Roosevelt could have done was to insist on an ironclad arrangement guaranteeing access to Allied ex-prisoners; they should have informed Stalin that repatriation would only proceed on a quid pro quo basis. The most the Western leaders could have done was to set up a trade-off in which British-American repatriation would occur, in exchange for access to Poland and a broadening of the Warsaw government.[55] Since the Soviet nationals, knowing of the fate awaiting them upon their return, frantically sought to remain in the west, Churchill and Roosevelt could not have been charged with holding hostages for diplomatic purposes. Indeed, returning people against their will in the interest of Soviet-American harmony amounted to trading in human flesh. In the final analysis, Roosevelt's contention that the Yalta accords were "the best he could do for Poland" would ring much truer if he had known what he could have tried.

Notes

[1]William Taubman, *Stalin's American Policy: From Entente to Detente to Cold War*, p. 61.

[2]Ibid., p. 56.

[3]Charles F. Delzell, "Russian Power in Central-Eastern Europe," in John L. Snell, ed., *The Meaning of Yalta: Big Three Diplomacy and the New Balance of Power*, p. 87.

[4]Taubman, *Stalin's American Policy*, p. 68.

[5]Lynn Etheridge Davis, *The Cold War Begins: Soviet-American Conflict over Eastern Europe*, pp. 197–98.

[6]Taubman, *Stalin's American Policy*, p. 68.

[7]John Erickson, *The Road to Berlin: Continuing the History of Stalin's War with Germany*, p. 270.

[8]Ibid., pp. 282–83.

[9]Herbert Feis, *Churchill-Roosevelt-Stalin: The War They Waged and the Peace They Sought*, p. 386. After this rejection President Roosevelt chose not to respond too vigorously because the United States was then carrying on conversations with the Soviets to gain access to airfields in the maritime provinces in the Far East. To do so could complicate those discussions. See Roosevelt to Churchill, August 26, 1944, Franklin D. Roosevelt Papers, Map Room File, Box 35, Folder 5.

[10]*Foreign Relations: Yalta*, p. 214.

[11]Taubman, *Stalin's American Policy*, p. 76.

[12]*Foreign Relations: Yalta*, pp. 217–18.

[13]Ibid., p. 224.

[14]Ibid., p. 231.

[15]Ibid., p. 234.

[16]Edward R. Stettinius, Jr., *Roosevelt and the Russians: The Yalta Conference,* pp. 88–89.

[17]*Foreign Relations: Yalta,* p. 590.

[18]Ibid., pp. 677–78.

[19]Ibid., pp. 678–79.

[20]Taubman, *Stalin's American Policy,* p. 92; *Foreign Relations: Yalta,* pp. 679–81.

[21]*Foreign Relations: Yalta,* p. 680.

[22]Ibid., p. 719.

[23]Ibid., p. 716.

[24]Ibid., pp. 717–20, 776–86.

[25]Feis, *Churchill-Roosevelt-Stalin,* p. 527.

[26]*Foreign Relations: Yalta,* pp. 803–04, 806.

[27]Ibid., pp. 850–52, 853–54.

[28]Winston S. Churchill, *The Second World War: Triumph and Tragedy,* p. 385; *Foreign Relations: Yalta,* p. 898.

[29]*Foreign Relations: Yalta,* pp. 973–74 (author's emphasis).

[30]George V. Kacewicz, *Great Britain, the Soviet Union and the Polish Government in Exile (1939–1945),* p. 211.

[31]*Foreign Relations: Yalta,* p. 973 (author's emphasis).

[32]Robert E. Sherwood, *Roosevelt and Hopkins: An Intimate History,* p. 898.

[33]*Foreign Relations: Yalta,* p. 788.

[34]George F. Kennan, *Memoirs,* 1:212.

[35]Ibid., p. 211.

[36]Mark R. Elliot, *Pawns of Yalta: Soviet Refugees and America's Role in Their Repatriation,* p. 8.

[37]See Russell D. Buhite, "Soviet-American Relations and the Repatriation of Prisoners of War, 1945," *The Historian* 35, no. 3 (May 1973): 384–86.

[38]Ibid., pp. 386–87; Elliot, *Pawns of Yalta,* pp. 36–37.

[39]*Foreign Relations: Yalta,* pp. 754–56.

[40]Elliot, *Pawns of Yalta,* p. 40.

[41]Buhite, "Soviet-American Relations," p. 388.

[42]Ibid.

[43]Harriman to Roosevelt, March 8, 1945, *Foreign Relations, 1945,* 5:1075.

[44]Ibid., p. 1078.

[45]Roosevelt to Stalin, March 17, 1945, ibid., p. 1082.

[46]Stalin to Roosevelt, March 22, 1945, ibid., p. 1083.

[47]Harriman to Roosevelt, March 24, 1945, ibid., p. 1086; Harriman to Stettinius, March 14, 1945, ibid., p. 1081.

[48]Churchill to Roosevelt, February 28, 1945, ibid., p. 132.

[49]Harriman to Roosevelt, March 8, 1945, ibid., p. 1075; ibid., pp. 134–44. See also Harriman to Roosevelt, March 12, 1945, ibid., p. 1078.

[50]Harriman to Stettinius, March 14, 1945, ibid., p. 1080; ibid.

[51]Stettinius to Roosevelt, ibid., p. 1079n; Roosevelt to Stalin, March 17, 1945, ibid., p. 1082.

[52]Harriman to Stettinius, April 7, 1945, ibid., p. 1090. See also Churchill to Roosevelt, March 16, 1945, ibid., pp. 171–72. If there was any thought on the part of Harriman, Deane, or Kennan to convert the prisoner contact groups into representatives of the Polish Commission, they never communicated it to Washington. Because of the specific duties of prospective prisoner contact teams and the fact that the United States had long been pressing the Soviets on the prisoner issue, there seems little reason to believe that American officials saw the two matters as anything but separate, although they obviously would not have been adverse to acquiring information about Poland from whatever source.

[53]Harriman to Stettinius, April 2, 1945, ibid., p. 1087; Harriman to Stettinius, June 11, 1945, ibid., p. 1097. Harriman's account is corroborated most poignantly by Svetlana Alliluyeva, who tells of a friend who was imprisoned for twelve years in a labor camp after being repatriated. Svetlana Alliluyeva, *Only One Year*, p. 268. See also Alexander Dallin, *German Rule in Russia*, p. 420.

[54]Elliot, *Pawns of Yalta*, p. 248.

[55]Ibid., p. 247.

IV
The United Nations

One of the issues that immediately strikes even the mildly observant student of World War II is that, despite the tremendous military pressure on the Soviet Union and the ensuing struggle for its very survival and, despite the fact that the Soviets needed the United States as much as the United States needed them, it was the latter that always sought to court the goodwill of the USSR and not the other way around. As on many other issues of wartime importance, American supplication suffused the Polish question. Nowhere, however, was the message so starkly conveyed that the United States required Soviet collaboration and friendship, rather than the converse, than on the planning for the new international organization.

A concept that began germinating almost immediately after Pearl Harbor, the United Nations gained motor force with the Declaration of the United Nations of January 1, 1942, which pledged its signatories to the principles of the Atlantic Charter, including the latter's provision that all nations be guaranteed security within their own boundaries. President Franklin Roosevelt began developing his ideas on the matter early in 1942. At first he thought that a concert of the major powers was the best vehicle for maintaining international security, and he conveyed his views to Soviet Foreign Minister Molotov in May of that year. Later he believed that the large powers could assume major responsibility for security, while a more general organization could take over nonsecurity duties, or such matters as those relating to health, education, nutrition, and economics.

In 1943 Roosevelt further expressed his ideas in an article by Forrest Davies published in the *Saturday Evening Post*. Despite the ignominious failure of the League of Nations, the president believed that the new organization should retain some of the League's provisions, especially the mandate, or trusteeship, system and the commissions designed to deal with specific economic and social matters. The Big Four powers would enforce the peace through the use of quarantine and military force, including preventive air power. Since the USSR would constitute the only military power in both Europe and Asia, Roosevelt considered it most important to secure Soviet cooperation in any postwar organization; otherwise, there was little hope of achieving success.

At least partially to assuage their frustrations at being consistently bypassed with regard to wartime decision making, Secretary Cordell Hull and State Department personnel threw themselves, with uncharacteristic boldness, into making plans for a postwar United Nations. The first formal department effort came with Hull's appointment in 1942 of an advisory committee on postwar foreign policy, which by June of that year began to devote its main attention to the problem of creating a permanent security organization. As chairman of this committee, Undersecretary of State Sumner Welles expressed sentiment in favor of a single world institution, in which regional groupings of the less powerful states would be subsumed in a sort of federated arrangement. The committee then put forward a plan for a provisional UN authority that would function until the war's end as a training agency for personnel of a more permanent organization. This provisional United Nations, whose membership would include all UN signatories, was to have a Security Council composed of the four major powers and representatives of other regional groups in which the major states would play the dominant role in security-related questions.

Hull did not like the proposals for regional groupings, and he did not trust Welles because of personal animosity, as well as the undersecretary's access to the president. Accordingly, he took over direction of the main State Department committee, which by the fall of 1943 had devised a plan for an international organization. The secretary then took the initiative at the Moscow Conference of October 1943 to secure agreement among the Allies for the creation of such a body. The Moscow Declaration stated that the Allies would make the organization open to "all peace-loving states" on the basis of "sovereign equality." Hull, ecstatic at his demarche, thereupon announced the end of spheres-of-influence and balance-of-power diplomacy.

Meanwhile, the British Foreign Office and Prime Minister Churchill began preliminary planning for a world organization. The Foreign Office expressed greater empathy toward the smaller nations than did Churchill, who, like Roosevelt, favored great-power domination. Churchill also advocated regional councils responsible for peacekeeping in their areas that would be subordinate to a world council. Unimpressed with the thought of a truly global organization, the prime minister expected a world body to consist of an association of the four allies and the continued close collaboration between the United States and Great Britain, even to the point of combined military chiefs of staff and common citizenship.

British planning was desultory, however, compared to the American, and a major part of the effort in the United States focused on avoiding the mistakes over the adoption of the League of Nations. This meant working closely with Congress, which in 1943 had passed the Fulbright Resolution in the House in September and the Connally Resolution in the Senate in November in support of U.S. involvement in an international organization. When Secretary Hull and his committee had completed a draft of the UN recommendations, the secretary gave them to the Senate Foreign Relations Committee for review and to a group of three political luminaries fo. their observations. The senators, including isolationist Arthur H. Vandenberg of Michigan, gave the State Department draft their tentative approval, although some objected to the veto provision in the Security Council.

Equally as important, Hull consulted with Republican presidential hopeful Thomas E. Dewey and his foreign policy expert, John Foster Dulles, to hear their opinions and to keep the matter out of the 1944 election. Both Dulles and Dewey endorsed the State Department proposals in the main, but they too had objections.

The veto power of the permanent members of the proposed Security Council occasioned the most discussion, both within the United States and among the United States and its wartime allies. By April of 1944, American officials had decided that the four main allies should comprise the permanent members of the UN Security Council, a body that would be enlarged by the election of other nonpermanent members through the General Assembly. On major questions, such as enforcement procedures, preservation of the peace, regulation of armaments, and the settlement of disputes, any one of the major powers could prevent action through a veto. That some U.S. policymakers desired the veto be absolute is evidenced by the suggestion that the great powers have this right even in disputes to which they were a party. Certainly, Hull himself believed that the veto was necessary for the United States on many issues.[1]

When the Dumbarton Oaks Conference convened at the Harvard University estate in Washington, DC, between August 21 and October 7, 1944, the matter received attention by British, Soviet, American, and Chinese delegates. (British, American, and Soviet delegates met from August 21 to September 28, and the Chinese joined the American and British delegates from September 29 to October 7.) Indicating their concern for the sensibilities of the smaller nations, the British delegates suggested that powers involved in a dispute should not be allowed to obstruct action by the Security Council by exercising a negative vote. Although many U.S. officials had earlier held the opposite view, the American delegation now sided with the British.

The Soviet leaders did not agree, arguing that unanimity of the major powers on all issues was essential before taking Security Council action. They also held to this position to the end of the conference in spite of American efforts to work out a compromise on voting procedures. Secretary of State Hull, with Roosevelt's support, concurred that, on matters involving the security of any one of the Big Four nations, the vote of the permanent members should be unanimous but would not go beyond that in meeting the Russian objection. As the conference adjourned, it appeared that the Soviets would refuse to participate in a general UN conference if they did not get their way on the voting issue.

The Soviets were equally obstinate about membership for sixteen Soviet republics in the new organization, claiming that these republics were autonomous units in foreign policy. In actuality, they were about as independent of the Kremlin as Pinocchio of Geppetto, and President Roosevelt quickly indicated that the United States would not go along. Even more, U.S. officials worked to keep the Soviet request secret in the belief that disclosure would outrage the American people, lead to criticism of the Soviet Union, and ultimately make the Soviets less willing to cooperate on a variety of issues. President Roosevelt, in any event, believed that he could negotiate a way around this problem when he had a chance to discuss it in person with Stalin.

Despite the failure to reach agreement on the aforementioned questions and on several others that the Allies would later address at Yalta, the powers on October 9 published the Dumbarton Oaks proposals, which recommended the establishment of a permanent international organization called the United Nations, which was to be available to all peace-loving states on the basis of sovereign equality. The United Nations would use collective measures to maintain peace and security; work to develop friendly relations among states; promote cooperation on economic, social, and humanitarian problems, and centralize the effort to harmonize the activities of all nations for the common good. The main organs of the new organization were to be the Security Council (composed of four permanent and seven other members elected for two-year terms), General Assembly, Secretariat, Economic and Social Council connected with the General Assembly, and the International Court of Justice. American officials expected that the General Assembly and the Economic and Social Council would somehow eliminate issues causing friction; the International Court of Justice would, if possible, settle disputes judicially; and the Security Council would put down aggression when it occurred.

In addition to the voting formula and membership for the Soviet republics, the delegates to Dumbarton Oaks left unresolved a number of questions that President Roosevelt would insist on dealing with at Yalta. Which nations were to attend the opening meeting of the United Nations and thus become original members? Where should the initial meeting take place? What should be done with the Japanese mandated islands in the Pacific that the United States would control when the war ended?

On the issue of the voting formula, which proved most difficult at the Crimean Conference, President Roosevelt had approved a compromise proposal in mid-November. Drafted by Alger Hiss, the State Department officer designated as a special assistant to work on UN matters, and sent out to Stalin and Churchill on December 5, this proposal recommended that the Security Council be able to settle procedural matters by a majority vote of seven members, but that on all other questions unanimity of the permanent members would be required. During the period that the Security Council worked at arranging a peaceful settlement of a dispute through advice, conciliation, or adjudication, any member of the council party to the dispute would refrain from voting. No American official, neither the president nor U.S. diplomats, offered a definition of what constituted a procedural question.[2]

Predictably, the Soviet leaders did not accept the proposal, arguing that it risked precipitating friction between the major powers. They refused to agree that the Security Council could act without the approval of all permanent members. What motivated Stalin and Molotov's reaction is unclear, but Ambassador Averell Harriman believed it was fear that their freedom of movement in neighboring countries would be impinged. It might be necessary for the Soviet Union to use coercion, even military force, in the revision of their western boundaries, and they did not want interference from a world body that was not likely to be impartial.[3] If the Soviets were strongly opposed, the British became almost as unenthusiastic about the plan, a fact that Prime Minister Churchill made plain before the Yalta Conference convened. The British soon came around to the American point of view, but it took longer to convince the Russians.[4]

Whether for negotiating purposes at the upcoming conference or as a sincere expression of his country's position, Soviet Ambassador to the United States Andrei Gromyko restated the Russian aversion to the voting formula on January 11, 1945, following up his statement with renewed insistence on extra votes for the Soviet Union in the world organization. Gromyko's argument on voting centered on the role to be played by the Security Council in settling disputes. He thought the body could and should *discuss* anything but should not act unless all the permanent members agreed. To the Soviets, the United Nations in its essence constituted a great-power concert, the main purpose of which was to protect the Soviet Union from aggression. At the same time, Gromyko defended his demand for sixteen votes for the Soviet republics by repeating the canard about their independence on foreign affairs matters, which again no one in Washington took seriously.

American officials saw some hope of negotiating on both of the above items. They were more alarmed by Soviet desires, which the Soviet ambassador passed along on January 13, for a share in the control of the Italian and Japanese colonies after the war was over. Gromyko seemed more interested in the UN trusteeship scheme than in anything else.

When the Yalta Conference opened, the Soviets for a time continued their opposition to the U.S. voting formula, despite the fact that Ambassador Gromyko saw clearly that it would create no problem for the Soviet Union. At a dinner on the evening of February 4, Churchill, Roosevelt, and Stalin engaged in an exchange over the amount of concern that the Big Three should show for the smaller powers. Stalin suggested that the smaller nations were expecting too much of the countries that were winning the war, to which Churchill offered the rejoinder that, while his colleague might be correct, the big powers should show respect and act moderately toward the small. This was Roosevelt's view, but to what degree the president wished the UN structure to reflect this concern is open to question. His proposal was patently designed to create the appearance of solicitude without surrendering any real power.[5]

Serious negotiations began on February 6 when Secretary of State Edward Stettinius presented the American formula, which remained essentially the same as the one sent to the British and Soviets on December 5. Although at first inclined to support the Soviet view on voting, a position that incidentally led to a spirited argument between himself and Foreign Minister Anthony Eden after dinner on February 4, Churchill now indicated that he enthusiastically favored the American plan. As he saw correctly, it did not diminish the power of the major allies to protect their interests.

Stalin acted as though he had a hard time believing the latter point but probably accepted the counsel of Gromyko that dissent would allow the Soviets to use the issue as a throwaway chip later on. To Churchill's admonition that, unless the Big Three made some concessions to the lesser nations, they would subject themselves to charges of attempting to rule the world, Stalin responded by acting insulted. Who was the prime minister suggesting in his comment about world domination, the Soviet ruler asked? If not Great Britain, and surely not the United States, he must mean the Soviet Union. This was a deliberate attempt to place Churchill on the defensive since not even the crudest logic could lead one to the conclusion that Churchill was accusing the Soviet Union. It is evident that, along with the Russian request for more time to study the proposal, members of the Soviet delegation wished to create the impression that they were making a major concession when they later accepted the formula. Secretary Stettinius did not believe for one minute that Stalin had failed to study it carefully in advance of the conference, nor would it have been in character for the Soviet leader and his delegation to fail to prepare themselves on an issue so important to the United States.[6]

What the American plan stated, and a point that the Yalta discussions of February 6 demonstrated, was that there were to be two ways for the Security Council to settle disputes, neither of which should cause worry for the Big Three. First was coercion, or the use of sanctions of some sort. In these cases, permanent members of the council could vote and thus veto action even if they were parties to a dispute. The second way was peaceful settlement. When the council was considering a peaceful settlement, a party to the dispute had to abstain from voting. Since peaceful solutions implied no action except the possible mobilization of opinion against a permanent member and anything beyond that could be prevented by the veto, there was adequate protection.

If Stalin had any concern it was about what mobilization of opinion could mean to the Soviets. He asked Churchill what would happen if Egypt demanded the Suez Canal or China Hong Kong. Both Egypt and China could secure other votes to support them. Churchill delivered a long discourse first on Hong Kong and then on the Suez in which he pointed out that, while either China or Egypt was free to discuss these issues in the General Assembly and could seek Security Council action, Great Britain could preclude any action against itself with a veto. Eden, Stettinius, and Roosevelt all agreed in effect that no enforcing power existed against the permanent members, nor was it possible to expel one of the Big Three as the League of Nations had done with the Soviet Union after it had invaded Finland. Expulsion was an action that any of the permanent members also could prevent with a veto.[7]

Stalin revealed his negotiating purposes during the fourth plenary session on February 7. In the middle of discussing the Polish question, during which Roosevelt and Churchill were pressing for the creation of an entirely new provisional government, the Soviet leader stopped the proceedings; stated that Foreign Minister Molotov had worked out some new proposals on the Polish question; and indicated that, since these proposals had not yet been typed, the Allies should first consider the Dumbarton Oaks formula. Molotov then suddenly announced that the Soviets would accept the U.S. position on voting; these, he said, "were entirely acceptable." More than that, the Soviets would no longer insist on having sixteen republics admitted as original members but would settle for just two or three.[8] This was only fair since the British Commonwealth countries would join as original members. Having made a "major concession" to the American and British position on the United Nations, Stalin undoubtedly hoped to gain easier acceptance of a simple broadening of the Lublin government, rather than a new provisional regime in Poland. Short of that, he wanted approval of his request for UN membership for the Soviet republics.

The effect of this ploy on Roosevelt and Churchill is unclear. President Roosevelt did suggest that Molotov's subsequent proposal on Poland represented "progress" when, in fact, it offered nothing substantially new.[9] The president was not ready immediately to concede the Soviet request on the republics, although his discussions later that evening with Secretary Stettinius indicate that he was leaning toward doing so. Prime Minister Churchill was anxious to make a friendly gesture toward the Soviets on UN membership, ironically in view of Stalin's own tactics because he wished to evoke from them more cooperation regarding Poland.[10]

Averring that "Great Britain could not agree to any organization which would reduce the status of the Dominions or exclude them from participation," Churchill informed his allies that equity also required membership for the Soviet republics.[11] The British would insist that five dominions, including India, be granted membership, in large part because of their major contribution in the war effort. Given that fact, the British could not in good conscience oppose the Soviet request.

During the plenary session of February 7, President Roosevelt had requested that the Allies remand the membership question to the foreign ministers for study. As preparation for the ministers' session, Hiss drafted a document for Stettinius's guidance, laying out reasons why the United States should oppose the Soviet request. However, before the foreign ministers met the next day, Roosevelt revealed his views to the secretary of state, arguing that since only the Security Council would have real power he doubted that a couple of extra votes in the General Assembly for the Soviet Union would make any difference. He also did not want to place himself in opposition to Churchill on the matter. Accordingly, at the next plenary session on the afternoon of February 8, Roosevelt told Stalin, even before he had formalized the American position with Stettinius and the State Department delegation, that the United States would accept membership of two extra Soviet republics.

Having given consent to the Soviet request, Roosevelt and Churchill found themselves faced with the vexing question of whether the Ukraine and White Russia, the extra Soviet republics, should attend the opening UN conference on world organization. The Allies agreed that those countries that had signed the Declaration of the United Nations by the time the Yalta meetings ended would receive an invitation to the opening conference. By agreement the conference would convene in San Francisco on April 25. Molotov and Stalin quickly asked that the Allies allow the Soviet republics to sign the declaration and thus join the opening meeting.

Roosevelt and Stettinius at this point found themselves in an awkward position because the American invitation list included the British Commonwealth nations and six Latin American countries, which had "associated" themselves with the UN declaration but not joined. (None of these countries had contributed significantly to the war effort.) Stalin reminded the president that the Soviet republics had borne some of the worst of the war with Germany, a fact that the U.S. delegation could not deny. Roosevelt, however, considered the extra votes for the Soviets a concession that did not reflect reality since the republics were not independent on foreign policy. Obviously he was correct in believing that they could not be considered in the same class with the British Commonwealth nations nor any of the smaller countries discussed for membership, including those from Latin America. He was not convinced that contribution in the war effort should constitute the main criterion for original membership.

Actually neither Churchill nor Roosevelt liked the idea, with the president asserting that it would create "difficulties," but both promised that they would support the later addition of the two republics at the first meeting. Persistent to the end, Molotov tried again to gain acceptance of the Soviet proposal on the last day of the conference, but Roosevelt would not agree.[12] As events transpired, the Soviets remained committed to the point even after the Yalta Conference ended and showed up at San Francisco with two extra delegations, much to the consternation of American officials. What worried President Roosevelt at Yalta was U.S. public reaction to three votes for the Soviet Union, six votes for Great Britain, and only one for the United States, and to have this highlighted at the opening session.

Roosevelt's anxiety derived in part from protest within the American delegation. James Byrnes, former senator from South Carolina and later secretary of state under President Harry S.

Truman, reminded Roosevelt that he had ridiculed the Soviet proposal to members of the Senate Foreign Relations Committee before his departure for Yalta. Both Byrnes and New York political boss Edward J. Flynn, whom Roosevelt took along to Yalta for reasons never adequately explained, complained that the Irish community in the major eastern cities would not understand the Allies, particularly the British, receiving more representation than the United States.[13] Nor would the American public generally fall for the fiction that the Soviet republics had true independence in foreign policy.

To cover himself in the event of a political storm in the United States, Roosevelt on February 10 wrote a letter to Stalin and Churchill in which he explained his potential embarrassment and asked their support for additional votes for the United States. This might be necessary, he stressed, to guarantee public and congressional assent to the extra representation for the British and Soviets. Both allies agreed to back the president's request, but the United States never chose to exercise the option.[14]

Perhaps because the British and Soviets did not value the United Nations so highly and were therefore willing to defer to the American position, the Yalta sessions on international organization remained remarkably free from controversy. One issue that did generate some heat, however, was that of UN trusteeships. On February 9 at the foreign ministers' session, Stettinius urged his colleagues to agree that invitations to the organization meeting include a statement that "the above-named governments have agreed that it would, in their opinion, be desirable that consideration be given at the forthcoming Conference to the inclusion of the projected charter of provisions relating to territorial trusteeships and dependent areas." Neither Eden, who knew how sensitive Churchill would become on this issue, nor Molotov would go along with the proposal.

Stettinius then brought the whole trusteeship matter before the heads of state that afternoon. Although President Roosevelt had ideas about the disposition of the British Empire, it was not his intention to create controversy or risk Allied harmony at this session; he wanted to limit the discussion to trusteeship arrangements for enemy territories. Either failing to understand this, or out of a desire to warn the United States to stay clear of the British Empire, Churchill exploded: "I will not have one scrap of British territory flung into that area. After we have done our best to fight in this war and have done no crime to anyone. I will have no suggestion that the British Empire is to be put into the dock." "Never, never, never," he protested further; "every scrap of territory over which the British flag flies is immune."[15] To this outburst Stalin responded gleefully, pacing up and down behind his chair and applauding. Roosevelt replied that when Stettinius finished his presentation the prime minister would see things more clearly, which as it turned out is exactly what happened. Once fully assured that only enemy territory was involved, he calmed down.

British protestations had their effect and ultimately found their way into the final conference documents. The Allies agreed that the five permanent members would consult before the opening UN conference to decide on machinery for establishing trusteeships. They also agreed to create trusteeships for only three categories of territories: existing League mandates, enemy territories, and other territories voluntarily surrendered.

Of all the issues discussed at Yalta, none raised the hopes of President Roosevelt and other American officials so high as the agreement on the United Nations. On no other issue were the results so illusory. Because of the inability to secure agreement at the Dumbarton Oaks Conference, members of the U.S. delegation went to Yalta skeptical of their chances to gain Soviet cooperation, the latter a necessary precondition to any successful international organization. When the Soviets accepted the entire American package, Roosevelt and Stettinius were ecstatic, hailing this acceptance as proof in itself of the success of the summit. The important question for the historian is: What was achieved? Stalin desired an international organization only insofar as it would serve as the vehicle for preserving Anglo-American-Soviet hegemony. For the Soviets this meant a sphere of influence in Eastern and Central Europe which the British and Americans, acting through the organization, would help guarantee.

That Stalin had no interest in establishing a body that would limit Soviet sovereignty or freedom of action goes without saying. He understood that neither the voting formula nor any other provision of the U.S. proposals at Yalta posed any threat whatsoever to the great powers that might themselves threaten international order. Roosevelt also understood this, but he had a great capacity to persuade both the American people and himself. He wanted an accord that would look good to the world and would begin the process of cooperation. He then convinced himself that the new organization, once launched, would have an organic quality, allowing it to grow into an instrument for lasting peace.

Notes

[1]John L. Snell, *The Meaning of Yalta: Big Three Diplomacy and the New Balance of Power*, pp. 14–19; Cordell Hull, *The Memoirs of Cordell Hull*, 2:1648, 1649–70; Harley Notter, ed., *Postwar Foreign Policy Preparation, 1939–1945*, pp. 247–69.

[2]*Foreign Relations: Yalta*, pp. 58–60, 684–86.

[3]Ibid., pp. 64–66.

[4]Ibid., p. 77.

[5]Ibid., pp. 589–91.

[6]Edward R. Stettinius, Jr., *Roosevelt and the Russians: The Yalta Conference*, pp. 143–50.

[7]*Foreign Relations: Yalta*, pp. 664–65, 685.

[8]Ibid., p. 712.

[9]Ibid., p. 716.

[10]Ibid., pp. 712–14.

[11]Ibid., p. 714.

[12]Snell, *The Meaning of Yalta*, pp. 184–85.

[13]In a long letter to his wife during the trip, Flynn failed to say why the president took him along. Edward J. Flynn Papers, Box 25, Franklin D. Roosevelt Library. In his memoirs, he wrote, however, that Roosevelt wanted him to obtain information on the degree to which the large Catholic populations in areas of Eastern Europe that would come under Soviet domination would be permitted to practice their faith. Edward J. Flynn, *You're the Boss*, p. 185.

[14]*Foreign Relations: Yalta*, pp. 966–68.

[15]Ibid., pp. 844, 856.

V
The Far East

Conventional wisdom suggests that the Yalta Far Eastern accord was rooted in realism, and that President Franklin Roosevelt's granting of extensive concessions to the Soviet Union in Northeast Asia, in return for Soviet entrance into the war against Japan, represented an eminently sensible arrangement in view of the then problematic nature of the atomic bomb and the need to save American lives. Moreover, this deal reflected the considered positions of the president's political and military advisers and resulted from spirited negotiations with the Soviet leadership, whose cooperation in the Pacific war it was necessary to secure.

That this interpretation is partially correct does not mean that it is a satisfactory depiction of what actually occurred. President Roosevelt and Premier Stalin did very little negotiating over the terms of Soviet entrance into the war, the president acceding to Russian demands after less than fifteen minutes of discussion, a discussion in which Prime Minister Churchill did not even participate. Whether it was necessary for the United States to grant the Kuril Islands to the Soviet Union, much less a sphere of influence in Manchuria which Roosevelt did without consulting the Chinese, is a point that deserves attention. So, too, does the issue of whether the president concluded the agreement primarily for the purpose of bringing the Soviets into the war, or whether his main objective was a Russian commitment to the government of Jiang Jieshi (Chiang Kai-shek). Furthermore, in view of the obvious interests of the Soviets in participating in the final defeat of Japan, could Roosevelt have asked the Russians to buy into the war in the form of more precise and definitive support of the Nationalists, rather than the other way around?

Any attempt to assess the East Asian decisions reached at Yalta must begin, of necessity, with a review of Soviet and American interests in the region and an account of prior discussions on Russian involvement in the Pacific war. Both nations had objectives that the future course of the war would influence. On the Continent the Soviets' interests included domination in Outer Mongolia and Sinkiang, as well as extensive influence in Manchuria. These were areas of long-standing concern for imperial Russia, which in the case of Manchuria found itself in bitter turn-of-the-century competition with the Japanese and the Western powers. That the Bolsheviks repudiated capitalist imperialism did not mean that they would reject the hard-won czarist concessions in Central and Northeast Asia. Indeed, although they expressed willingness in 1924 to recognize Chinese sovereignty, by the 1930s the Soviets had achieved hegemony in Outer Mongolia, in effect making it a satellite state. In Manchuria, Stalin's postwar objectives coincided almost exactly with those of his czarist predecessors in that he wanted a naval base, a commercial port, and guaranteed access to the region's two major railroad systems.

If the Soviets sought the extension of their influence on the Continent, they were equally desirous of protecting the naval approaches to their empire. Because the island covered the mouth of the Amur River and much of the coast of the Maritime Province, this meant the reacquisition from Japan of all of Sakhalin. The Soviets' strategic net also extended to the Kuril chain to the north and east of Japan.

Apart from the total defeat and demilitarization of Japan, the main American interest lay in establishing a stable, unified, and non-Communist China that would assume a position of postwar dominance in Asia. This interest arose not only out of U.S. economic and cultural involvement dating from the eighteenth and nineteenth centuries, but it also derived from the American desire to create a situation in Asia most conducive to lasting peace.

In the effort to defeat the Japanese, American planners had long believed that Soviet assistance would prove beneficial, if not essential, and they had tried on numerous occasions before Yalta to secure Stalin's promise of entrance into the war. Filled with hatred toward the perpetrators of the Pearl Harbor attack, many Americans wanted to prosecute the war against Japan as the first priority effort. President Roosevelt and his advisers rejected this approach in favor of an attempt to help sustain the British and Soviets in their desperate struggle against Hitler.

But, as early as December 1941, the president asked Soviet Ambassador Maxim Litvinov to encourage Moscow to join in the Far Eastern war immediately. The government of Jiang in China, reeling under the effects of Japanese occupation, seconded the motion.

In the following two years, U.S. officials pressed the issue, with some degree of success but without securing a firm commitment. During a visit to Moscow in November 1942, presidential envoy Patrick J. Hurley pointedly asked Stalin when he would be prepared to enter. Stalin responded that he recognized the importance of defeating Japan and, Hurley reported, "at one point his discussion indicated that Russia intended in due course to cooperate in the establishment of a mainland front against Japan."[1] This seems to have been the first indication by Stalin that his country would join the war, but it obviously fell short of what the United States wanted. The Soviet leader came closer to a commitment at the Moscow Foreign Ministers' Conference in October 1943, stating that soon after the defeat of Germany the USSR would enter. At the Tehran Conference two months later, the Soviets expanded on their pledge and, in their comments about Dairen and the Manchurian railways, began indicating the price they would expect to extract.

More serious negotiations began in 1944. In February of that year, Ambassador Averell Harriman pressed Stalin to allow planning to begin between Soviet and American military authorities, only to be told that such talks were premature. Soviet forces in the Far East were insufficient to contemplate war with Japan, Stalin argued, and the Soviets would require the rebuilding of their air force and the transfer of four infantry units from Europe before they would be ready. Perhaps by summer he could make a commitment. Thereafter, Harriman on several occasions asked Molotov when the head of the Soviet Far Eastern Air Force would be in Moscow to discuss the possible location of U.S. airfields on Soviet territory, either on Kamchatka Peninsula or near Vladivostok. Molotov refused to comment.

Compounding the frustration of U.S. officials, the Soviets on March 30 concluded two new agreements with Japan. One constituted a pledge by the Japanese to terminate their interests and involvement in the northern section of Sakhalin Island, while the other dealt with mutual fishing rights in Northeast Asian waters. Obviously these agreements led to speculation among

American policymakers as to whether the Soviets would follow through on their offer to help defeat Japan. Certainly, U.S. officials had every right to believe that the Soviets would enter the war on their own timetable, one that allowed them to build up their forces in the Far East, with American assistance, and then, once they took military action, to maximize their territorial gains in the region.[2]

Although Stalin responded more favorably during the summer of 1944, he still refused to be pinned down. He did promise that American bomber forces would be permitted to use air bases near Vladivostok, and he hoped that the United States would begin stocking supplies for the Soviets. He also told Harriman that the Soviets would gladly accept several hundred U.S. four-engine bombers for their Far Eastern Air Force. Stalin, however, seemed convinced that the United States wanted to provoke war between Japan and the Soviet Union through a Japanese attack on Russian interests in Northeast Asia. Thus he remained cautious and uncommunicative until fall.

In September, Stalin became concerned that the United States might withdraw its request. Feigning injury at the failure of American and British officials to mention Soviet participation in the Quebec Conference report, he sarcastically informed Harriman that, "if the United States and Great Britain desired to bring the Japanese to their knees without Russian participation, the Russians were ready to do this."[3] When Harriman assured him that the United States and Britain could hardly discuss Soviet involvement until the Soviets expressed a willingness to move ahead with planning, Stalin readily agreed to set things in motion. He moved quickly to try to summon his Far Eastern commanders to Moscow, where they began talks with General John Deane in early October.

Harriman and Deane extracted more specific commitments from Stalin in October. Deane informed the Soviet leader that American military officials hoped that the Soviets would play an important part in the defeat of Japan. This would include placing Soviet and American air bases in the Maritime Province, securing eastern Siberia and the Trans-Siberian Railroad, shutting off shipping between the Continent and Japan, and defeating Japan's forces in Manchuria. Stalin evaded answers to many U.S. queries, but he responded to General Deane's direct question as to the length of time the Soviets would need before declaring war on Japan. Russia, he said, would enter the war three months after the defeat of Germany, the period required to increase the number of divisions in Northeast Asia from thirty to sixty, if the United States could build up supplies for sixty divisions and if it could meet certain political conditions.[4]

These political conditions foreshadowed the Yalta agreement. Stalin informed Harriman in mid-October that he would require American approval of concessions to the Soviet Union as a precondition of entry. Although he did not at that time spell out exactly what the Soviets would demand, Stalin was referring to those provisions he had mentioned to President Roosevelt at Tehran, including access to the Manchurian ports and railroads. In a further meeting on December 14, Stalin told Harriman specifically that the Soviets wished to lease the ports on the Liaotung Peninsula as well as the Chinese Eastern Railway. He went on to add a new condition in which the Soviets would insist on acceptance of the status quo in Outer Mongolia.[5] If American officials ever had any hope that the Soviets would enter as the United States had done against Germany, assuming that all territorial questions would be solved after the war was over, they were fully disabused of the notion after the Harriman-Stalin talks. Interestingly, neither Harriman nor General Deane, who was also present at the October meeting, made any attempt to protest the Soviet leader's comments, although Harriman suggested in December the internationalizing of the ports.

President Roosevelt apparently resigned himself to paying Stalin's price. Why this was so is difficult to discern. The best guess is that it probably seemed necessary to have a firm understanding with the Soviets on the extent of their claims before their entrance because, as Stalin told Harriman, Soviet armies would range over northern China including the Peking area. President Roosevelt also had in mind a trade-off in which he would secure a Soviet pledge of support for Jiang's government. In other words, he was willing to pay the price to guarantee a postwar non-Communist China.

As U.S. officials prepared for the Yalta meetings, they did so knowing of Soviet verbal commitments. Stalin had promised to enter the war shortly after the defeat of Germany, and he gave tacit agreement to American military requirements in the Far East. Furthermore, he had stated on several occasions that he supported Jiang as the only logical leader in China. In return, the United States indicated a readiness to provide huge amounts of supplies for Soviet Far Eastern armies and to satisfy Stalin's political objectives. Apart from the State Department memoranda on Sakhalin and the Kuril Islands, which were not in his possession, President Roosevelt had with him at Yalta the studied recommendations of his advisers on the aforementioned political questions.

It is often noted that the Soviets bore the major burden in the defeat of Germany, and that they inflicted six times as many casualties on German forces as their Western allies, while undergoing immense suffering and hardship at home. Western delays in undertaking a major second front not only allowed the Soviets to take up favorable strategic positions in Eastern Europe but also gave them ground for their claim that their disproportionate share of the load in winning the war should bring a disproportionate share in the fruits of victory. There is no gainsaying that the strength of their contribution gave the Soviets the upper hand as the Yalta conferees dealt with European questions. One of the ironies of the Crimean Conference is that the United States occupied a similar position on Far Eastern matters but did not have as much success translating the strategic advantage into political gain.

If the United States and the British were reluctant to open a second front in Europe, the Soviet Union proved equally reluctant to open a front in Asia. The record of the Soviet-Japanese relationship demonstrates that the Soviet Union had a vital interest in the destruction of Japanese power, and the Japanese move into Southeast Asia cut off Western access to that important raw material region. The Pacific and European wars were inextricably linked in a number of ways, but only the United States and Great Britain recognized the fact by waging war against Germany's axis partner. Only the United States, while simultaneously providing large-scale Lend-Lease supplies to its allies, engaged in a major military effort against Japan. From April 1941 onward, when they signed a neutrality pact with Japanese Foreign Minister Yosuke Matsuoka, the Soviets let the United States deal with the mutual Far Eastern enemy.

Although Japan's defeat did not coincide with the opening of the Yalta Conference, it was much closer than American military leaders thought at the time. Japanese reports of "smashing victories" documented that these victories were occurring closer and closer to home. By February 6 the United States had established a forward line that included Attu at the end of the Aleutians to the Marianas Islands and Luzon in the Philippines. More importantly, the United States exercised sea and air control as far as China, Taiwan, the Ryukyus, and even the coast of Japan itself. In the near future, American forces would take the Bonin Islands and Okinawa, from which bases it would be possible to intensify the sea and air blockade. American bombers already were hitting the northern Kuriles from bases in the Aleutians, and a recent bombing attack conducted by 120 planes had devastated Kobe. The Japanese navy and merchant marine had been severely depleted, American power having so weakened the navy that it could no longer conduct a major battle.[6] The aforementioned U.S. military successes, not to mention the capture of Manila while the Crimean meetings were under way, were making Soviet entrance into the war less and less necessary.

That is not to say that the United States would fail to promote Soviet-American military cooperation in the Pacific conflict. Military leaders, either out of worst-case planning or bureaucratic determinism, remained committed to soliciting Soviet support, and they began discussions with their Soviet counterparts at Yalta several days before President Roosevelt and Stalin dealt with Far Eastern questions. These negotiations were a logical extension of the talks held in Moscow with Harriman, Deane, and Stalin.

The U.S. Joint Chiefs of Staff initiated contact with Soviet military officials on February 3, contact that they followed up nearly each day thereafter. On February 5 they began work on a memorandum outlining U.S. inquiries regarding air bases in Siberia and a supply line across the Pacific. Then on February 6 they sketched out, for the Soviet and British Chiefs of Staff, the military situation in the Pacific. If the U.S. Joint Chiefs thought that this openness would elicit a similar Soviet response, they were disappointed, for General of the Army Alexei Antonov refused to discuss any details until his superior had given him approval, which meant until Stalin had obtained an agreement with Roosevelt. Nevertheless, the Joint Chiefs secured agreement from Antonov on February 7 for a meeting the following day which would focus on a number of strategic and tactical questions.

American military planners needed decisions on Soviet-American military coordination. Would the Soviets require a Pacific supply route after entering the war? Would the Soviets give approval to the operation of U.S. air forces in the Komsomolsk-Nikolayevsk area near the Amur River in eastern Siberia? Would U.S. forces be required for the defense of

Kamchatka? Would the Soviets occupy Sakhalin Island, how soon, and would they secure the strait between Sakhalin and Hokkaido? Would the Soviets follow combined planning in Moscow? Would they provide more weather information from eastern Siberia? Finally, would the Soviets honor their pledge to enter the war approximately three months after Germany's defeat?

After discussion with Stalin, Antonov replied on February 8 that the Soviets would abide by their commitment of October 1944. They also would try to keep the Trans-Siberian Railroad in operation but would require that supply routes across the Pacific remain open. Rather than provide construction and storage of supplies for the United States, the Soviets would probably request that the United States build fuel storage for Russian forces. When the Soviets occupied Sakhalin Island, they would do so themselves without U.S. assistance, and they would not allow the United States to traverse the strait between Sakhalin and Hokkaido, at least until they had established a naval base there. While the Soviets tried to coordinate military activity with American forces, questions concerning the basing of American forces in Siberia, or the entry of U.S. survey groups into Kamchatka, would be deferred until Stalin had a chance to examine them.[7]

Having consulted more fully with his superior, General Antonov gave definitive replies to the American Joint Chiefs on February 9, answers in which, for the most part, he simply reconfirmed his statements of the previous day. To the American request for an air base in the Kamchatka-Nikolayevsk area he was evasive but agreed to consign the matter to the respective air staffs for discussion after the main military conference ended. When General Lawrence S. Kuter remarked during these talks that the U.S. requirement would be for two large bases to accommodate B-29s, his Russian counterpart was taken aback, thereby signaling that this was an American request that Stalin would put off and then deny completely. Earlier, General Antonov had specified that the sending of a U.S. survey team to Kamchatka must be deferred until the last minute, ostensibly to keep the Japanese in the dark about American-Soviet plans.[8]

U.S.-Soviet military discussions resolved many of the difficult issues, thus setting the stage for the final report of the Anglo-American Combined Chiefs of Staff on February 9, a document reflecting the pessimism of Allied military planners and rationalizing the Far Eastern political settlement. Convinced that it would be necessary to invade and occupy the industrial heart of

Japan, the Chiefs of Staff believed that even with Russian assistance the end of the war would not come soon. "We recommend," they wrote, "that the planning date for the end of the war against Japan should be set at eighteen months after the defeat of Germany."[9]

Historians have argued that the expectation of a long and bloody struggle for control of Japan proper underlay the American acquiescence in Stalin's political demands. The evidence suggests, however, that Roosevelt did not make the Far Eastern agreement primarily for military purposes. The president was ahead of his military advisers in recognizing that the United States probably would not require Soviet intervention, nor would it have to take the losses anticipated in carrying the war to the home islands. He revealed his reasoning when he informed Stalin on February 8 that he hoped it would now be possible, by "intensive bombing," to destroy Japan and its army and thus save American lives. Roosevelt would invade the homeland "only if absolutely necessary."[10] If, as he anticipated, the United States could bomb Japan into submission, then Soviet military support obviously would become only a tertiary concern.

How Roosevelt thought the United States would destroy Japan through the air becomes more understandable in context of two developments. He knew the air war against Japan had been, and would continue to be, successful, and he received a report on the atomic bomb at the end of December. Conventional textbook accounts of the Yalta decisions note that lack of knowledge concerning the availability of the bomb or bombs, information which was not known until July 1945, impelled American officials to deal generously with the Soviets. This is not entirely accurate. General Leslie R. Groves, commander of the Manhattan Project, on December 30 gave General George Marshall a memorandum, which he quickly communicated to the president, stating that a bomb would be ready for use by the summer of 1945. "It is now reasonably certain," the document asserted, "that our operation plans should be based on the gun type bomb, which it is estimated, will produce the equivalent of a ten thousand ton T.N.T. explosion. The first bomb, without previous full scale test which we do not believe will be necessary, *should be ready about 1 August 1945*. The second one should be ready by the end of the year." President Roosevelt told Secretary of State Stettinius about the bomb several weeks before their departure for Yalta. Other information available to the president and to Stettinius certified that not only would the bomb be available by August 1945, but also that "it would explode," and its explosion "would wreck a large city."[11]

Accounts to the contrary notwithstanding, it seems highly unlikely that the information at his disposal could have left any doubt in Roosevelt's mind that the bomb would be available and would be extremely destructive, and that the United States would have use of one bomb, and perhaps more, before the Soviets entered the war. He knew the latter because of Soviet intimations that it would be three months after Germany's defeat before they came in, an interval that, even allowing for the most optimistic assessment of events in Europe, would place Russian partici- pation well after August 1, 1945. Assuming that Roosevelt believed Soviet entrance could still be useful in clearing out the Japanese from Manchuria, logic suggests that he would not make extensive concessions of Chinese possessions for such marginal assistance.

Why then did Roosevelt conclude the agreement? The Yalta Far Eastern accord can be better understood against the back- ground of U.S. objectives in China and President Roosevelt's attempt to construct a "large policy" that would enable the United States, with Soviet compliance, to promote a strong, non- Communist, postwar China.

American involvement in China during the war had both military and political dimensions. Militarily, the United States had hoped to achieve several goals that would prove helpful in the defeat of Japan. The optimum objective was that Jiang's armies, through intensive training and with American supplies, would revitalize themselves and inflict heavy casualties on Jap- anese troops in China. Even if Chinese forces did not win a clear victory, they could at least weaken the Japanese, making the invasion of Japan that much easier.

Short of decisive military success, U.S. officials hoped that Chinese armies could clear out the invading army from a large portion of the eastern coastal area, which, until the island hop- ping campaign proved so successful, the United States expected to use as staging bases for air attacks on Japan. The minimum objective was that China at least remain in the war because a Japanese victory would allow the transfer of hundreds of thou- sands of troops, either to the Pacific islands or to Japan proper, where they would impede the American offensive and lengthen the war.

Politically, the United States wanted a strong, stable, demo- cratic, and unified country, one capable of supplanting Japan as the dominant power in Asia and one susceptible to at least a measure of U.S. influence. Although the China market had never developed in the way turn-of-the-century traders had hoped it would, American officials also expected to gain increased access for U.S. commerce and investment. Both the political and military objectives required that China achieve a resolution of the plethora of internal problems it faced: runaway inflation, ill-trained armies, corrupt practices by all manner of government officials, inept military commanders, famine, disease, and, most importantly, the seething, debilitating conflict with the Communists.

To assist the Chinese government in achieving military efficiency, President Roosevelt sent General Joseph W. Stilwell to China as commander in chief of U.S. forces in the China-Burma-India theater and as Allied chief of staff under President Jiang. Stilwell tried without success to pressure Jiang into reorganizing and upgrading his forces. He insisted, also without success, that Jiang stop using Nationalist armies to block the Communists and to encourage the latter to attack the Japanese in northern China. Finally, when the substantive and personal issues between himself and the American general became too bitter, Jiang, in the fall of 1944, asked for Stilwell's recall.

Meanwhile, because he considered it so important, both in the continuation of the war effort and to the postwar situation, President Roosevelt sent Hurley, his personal emissary, to China in the summer of 1944 to help work out a unification agreement between the Communists and the Nationalists. In sending Hurley to China, Roosevelt recognized that the attitude of the Soviet Union toward the Chinese government and the Communists was vital in promoting the American program. Roosevelt understood that the United States would have to support the Chinese government, and that it could not be impartial in China's internal quarrel for three reasons: Jiang's government had gained stature in the United States and in world councils during the war; the United States desired a non-Communist China; and impartiality would have required military aid to the Communists, which would have made them less willing to compromise. In view of these constraints, it was necessary to guarantee the nonsupport of Mao Zedong's (Mao Tse-tung) cause by the Soviet Union. In effect, then, Roosevelt set out to establish a policy in which the United States would serve as a mediator between the Soviets and Jiang's government.

American efforts to draw the Soviet Union into its program had begun in the summer of 1944. On June 10, Ambassador Harriman extracted from Stalin a general statement of endorsement of Jiang's leadership, and in his trip to China that same month Vice President Henry A. Wallace informed the Generalissimo of Stalin's comments to Harriman. Then Hurley, with the president's authorization, stopped over in Moscow on his way to Chungking for the purpose of further determining Soviet views. Satisfied with Molotov's assurances that the Soviets would support the Chinese government, Hurley in October began the impossible task of forging a unification agreement. This effort was still going on when the Big Three met at Yalta.

Given the Soviet commitment in October to enter the Far Eastern war, and Stalin's ominous comment that Soviet forces would push far into China, it became even more necessary toward the end of 1944 to spell out precisely the Soviet relationship with the Jiang regime. If the Soviets advanced too far, in the absence of such an agreement or without a CCP-Guomindang accord, they might be tempted to act opportunistically and aid the Communists. It was therefore necessary, totally apart from the military requirements of the war against Japan, to have a Far Eastern agreement with the Soviet Union.

Serious discussion of the terms of this agreement began on February 8, in personal meetings between President Roosevelt and Stalin. Present at this first session were Ambassador Harriman, who a few days before had briefed Roosevelt on Stalin's prospective territorial demands, and Charles E. Bohlen, who acted as interpreter for the president. Foreign Minister Molotov and interpreter Vladimir Pavlov joined Stalin on the Soviet side. Interestingly, while Molotov participated in the meetings, Secretary Stettinius did not, which may be considered as commentary on President Roosevelt's attitude toward the State Department generally and toward Stettinius's abilities specifically.[12]

After discussing a number of military questions, including the building of air bases on Soviet territory and the transfer of ships to the Soviet Union after the war was over, Roosevelt and Stalin settled down to their talks on the political conditions of Russian entry. Stalin took the initiative, explaining to the president that he already had had a conversation with Harriman on this issue. Roosevelt quickly followed this initial exchange by laying his cards on the table. He had no difficulty, he said, with

Stalin's request for the southern half of Sakhalin Island and the Kuriles.[13] Whether he might have had difficulty had he known of a State Department memorandum dated December 28 on the disposition of the Kuriles is an interesting point. In any event, his statement conceded the Kuriles to postwar Soviet control. Roosevelt went on to remind Stalin of his suggestion at Tehran that the Soviets receive access to a warmwater port at the end of the South Manchurian Railway, possibly at Dairen. Although he had not consulted Jiang, and at this point hesitated to obligate the Chinese, the president thought there were two possible methods for granting use of this port to the Soviets: outright leasing or making it an internationalized free port. He preferred the latter because he also hoped, but had not yet told Churchill, to encourage the British to do the same thing with Hong Kong.

Stalin also wanted railroads. The czars had had use of rail lines running from Manchouli to Harbin to Nikolsk-Ussurisk, and the Soviets desired the same privileges. To Roosevelt's response that direct leasing would be one way to do this while another, and from his point of view a better choice, would be a joint Sino-Soviet commission, Stalin riposted vigorously. It was clear to him that, if these conditions were not met, "it would be difficult for him and Molotov to explain to the Soviet people why Russia was entering the war against Japan." Since neither the destruction of the peasants, nor the purging of his old Bolshevik comrades and the major portion of his military officer corps, had caused him any problem in his explanation, it is hard to imagine how he kept a straight face. He went on to say that people "would not understand why Russia would enter a war against a country with which they had no great trouble," unless the political conditions were met, at which point they would see the national interest involved. Moreover, at that point "it would be very much easier to explain the decision to the Supreme Soviet."[14]

In the exchange over the railroads, as well as in the one over the ports, President Roosevelt invoked the Chinese. He had not consulted Jiang on the subject of the railroads, and he was reluctant to do so because anything said to Jiang's government "was known to the whole world in twenty-four hours." Stalin did not worry too much about security but agreed that it was not necessary at that time to speak to the Chinese. Perhaps later, when it was possible to transfer as many as twenty-five divisions to the Far East, Jiang could be told of what the Soviets and the Americans had done. In the meantime, to what must have been the great amusement of Harriman and Bohlen, Stalin said that he could "guarantee the security of the Supreme Soviet!" The Soviet leader was anxious to have the agreement in writing and urged that the three powers commit the conditions to paper before leaving Yalta. Roosevelt readily acceded to this request.[15]

While President Roosevelt during this conversation did not make a major issue of the China question, he let Stalin know that it was on his mind. He also informed the Soviet leader that General Albert C. Wedemeyer and Ambassador Hurley were having more success than their predecessor team had had in bringing the Communists and the Chinese government together. Then, in a transparent gesture to Stalin, Roosevelt pointed out that "the fault lay more with the Kuomintang and the Chungking Government than with the so-called communists." Stalin fell right in step, agreeing that President Jiang "should assume leadership" of a united front, which was exactly what Roosevelt wanted to hear.[16]

Having achieved basic acquiescence from President Roosevelt in their territorial demands during the exploratory discussions of February 8, the Soviet leaders sought a formal agreement on February 10, the next to the last day of the conference. Molotov presented Harriman with a draft proposal which stated, among other things, that Port Arthur and Dairen should be restored under lease to the Soviet Union. It was as though Roosevelt had spoken to the wall when he suggested that the ports be placed under international control. The draft also stated that the Soviets would recognize Chinese sovereignty in Manchuria but would receive the right to operate the Chinese Eastern and South Manchurian railways as the czarist government had done. To Harriman's response that the ports be free and internationalized, and that the railroads be run by a Soviet-Chinese commission, Molotov agreed, although with the kind of conviction that would allow for further maneuver. The Soviet foreign minister also consented to Harriman's reminder that the agreement on the ports and railways would require Jiang's concurrence.

Roosevelt approved the Soviet draft, with Harriman's amendments, but the Russians were not finished. On the afternoon of February 10, Prime Minister Churchill supported Stalin's expressed desire for a naval base at Port Arthur, declaring that the British would have no objection to stationing a Soviet fleet in the Pacific. Despite Molotov's "commitment" to internationalization, Stalin, strengthened by Churchill's comments, then told Harriman that, since the Russians required a naval base at Port Arthur, international control was possible only at Dairen.

In their final discussion of Far Eastern matters, Roosevelt and Stalin engaged in some trading. Roosevelt agreed that Port Arthur would be leased to the Soviet Union, while Stalin accepted the American position to create a Sino-Soviet commission for operating the railroads. The Soviet leader then asked for a guarantee of the status quo in Outer Mongolia, but this would require Jiang's approval, which the president indicated a willingness to secure at the proper moment. Indeed, all of the arrangements, save those dealing with Japanese territory, would require Chinese consent. To keep the agreement secret from the Japanese, Roosevelt would approach Jiang, the two leaders agreed, only when Stalin gave his approval.

These negotiations completed, the Allies were prepared to sign the final agreement, which the Soviets brought forward on February 11. Even though Churchill had not participated in most of the talks, and was advised against signing by Foreign Minister Eden, he added his signature to the document. Its terms are as follows:

> The leaders of the three Great Powers—the Soviet Union, the United States of America and Great Britain—have agreed that in two or three months after Germany has surrendered and the war in Europe has terminated the Soviet Union shall enter into the war against Japan on the side of the Allies on condition that:
>
> 1. The *status quo* in Outer-Mongolia (The Mongolian People's Republic) shall be preserved;
>
> 2. The former rights of Russia violated by the treacherous attack of Japan in 1904 shall be restored, viz:
>
> (a) the southern part of Sakhalin as well as all the islands adjacent to it shall be returned to the Soviet Union,
>
> (b) the commercial port of Dairen shall be internationalized, the preeminent interests of the Soviet Union shall be safeguarded and the lease of Port Arthur as a naval base of the USSR restored,
>
> (c) the Chinese-Eastern Railroad and the South-Manchurian Railroad which provides an outlet to Dairen shall be jointly operated by the establishment of a joint Soviet-Chinese Company it being understood that the preeminent interests of the Soviet Union shall be safeguarded and that China shall retain full sovereignty in Manchuria;
>
> 3. The Kuril Islands shall be handed over to the Soviet Union.

It is understood, that the agreement concerning Outer-Mongolia and the ports and railroads referred to above will require concurrence of Generalissimo Chiang Kai-shek. The President will take measures in order to obtain this concurrence on advice from Marshal Stalin.

The Heads of the three Great Powers have agreed that these claims of the Soviet Union shall be unquestionably fulfilled after Japan has been defeated.

For its part the Soviet Union expresses its readiness to conclude with the National Government of China a pact of friendship and alliance between the USSR and China in order to render assistance to China with its armed forces for the purpose of liberating China from the Japanese yoke.[17]

Hurriedly considered and vaguely worded, the Far Eastern document received the divided attention of statesmen who were trying to wrap up hundreds of other issues during the closing hours of the conference. Roosevelt was anxious to leave to keep his date with three kings in the Middle East, whom he had arranged to meet on his way home. Subordinates had worked all night preparing formal papers, which the three allies shuffled among their plates at the luncheon table on the 11th as they completed their business.

In the name of secrecy the accord was kept separate from the official protocol and from the joint communiqué released at the end of the conference. President Roosevelt also kept it from Congress when he made his report to that body on March 1, stating in regard to the Pacific only that the combined British and American Chiefs of Staff had held meetings at Malta to plan increased attacks on Japan. He made no comment on the political arrangements with the Soviets for their entrance into the war. Indeed, U.S. officials did not release the text of the agreement until early 1946.

That some degree of secrecy was necessary and defensible, few historians would dispute. Certainly it seems wise in retrospect to have avoided an open debate in Congress on the merits of the agreement because such a debate might have led to major Allied differences in Europe. Assuming that Roosevelt saw some military benefit in having the Soviets help remove the Japanese from Manchuria, it also made sense to avoid tipping off the Japanese about an impending attack. At the same time, however, it is hard to justify, on moral and ethical grounds, keeping the terms of the accord from Jiang, whose government would be called upon to make the sacrifice of territory. Moreover, secrecy had serious political consequences because it gave the later critics of the Roosevelt-Truman China policy an issue to exploit.

Secrecy aside, the agreement itself contained a number of important flaws. Its language was terribly imprecise, leaving unclear exactly what its parties meant when they said the "preeminent interests" of the Soviet Union would be safeguarded in the running of the Manchurian railways and in guaranteeing access to Dairen. The result was that the Soviets could, and did, insist in their later negotiations with Jiang's government on receiving dominant control of the railroads, Dairen, and Outer Mongolia. The agreement also reflected President Roosevelt's innocence of the State Department's 28 December memorandum on the Kuril Islands which would have precluded the transfer of all of that archipelago to the Soviet Union. This study, the work of Professor George H. Blakeslee of Clark University, stated that, while the Soviets had a substantial claim to the northern islands and some strategic claim to the central group, they had no solid ground for requesting the southern islands. Moreover, to transfer the southern islands, which were ethnically Japanese, to the Soviet Union would create a revanchist issue for Japan and deprive the Japanese of important fisheries. Despite Soviet claims to the north and central islands, Blakeslee's recommendation concluded that the strategic proximity of the archipelago to the Aleutian chain required that the entire chain be internationalized.[18]

There were perhaps better reasons to grant the Soviets the southern half of Sakhalin Island, which Russia had lost to the Japanese in the war of 1904–05, but President Roosevelt was likewise unaware of a State Department recommendation on Sakhalin. This document, like the one on the Kuriles, was not included in the Yalta briefing book. Largely the work of Japan expert Professor Hugh Borton, this memorandum urged that southern Sakhalin be made an international trusteeship in view of its importance to both Russia and Japan.[19] Whether the Soviets would have accepted anything less than control of either Sakhalin or the Kuriles depended on the force with which Roosevelt might have tried to make the American case. It is doubtful that the president would have chosen to resist Soviet entreaties over these territories since no one in February of 1945 was much inclined to preserve Japanese possessions. One can argue, however, as a prominent diplomatic historian has done, that "it was a mistake to allow the Soviet act of expansion to be phrased as a gesture of fair redress for past injuries."[20]

On this latter point, it is significant to reiterate that it was in the Soviets' interest to enter the war against Japan; indeed, Stalin worried that the war might end before they could do so. The Soviet ruler became aware in January of Japanese "peace feelers" to the United States which were being sent out through the pope, and later he learned of Japanese contact with American diplomats in Bern, Lisbon, and Stockholm. In fact, the vehemence of his response in April 1945 to hearing about German contact with the Office of Strategic Services in Bern with regard to a deal to surrender in Italy may have occurred in part as a result of his concern over a separate peace with Japan. That he continued to berate Roosevelt, even after receiving information corroborating the president's assurances that there was no "double dealing," suggests that Stalin hoped, by creating a row over this European question, to head off any U.S. attempt to negotiate with Japan. On May 11, Ambassador Harriman reported his belief that Stalin "feared a separate peace by ourselves with Japan," and Stalin's talks with Harry Hopkins later that month confirmed that the Soviets saw Japanese initiatives as "troublesome."[21]

If it was in the Soviets' interest to enter the war, and if they worried about a termination of the conflict before they jumped in, it follows that their entrance did not have to be purchased. Ambassador William Standley had told President Roosevelt in 1943 that "I don't think you can keep Stalin out." British Foreign Minister Eden had remarked in early 1945 that he thought paying any price for Soviet involvement in a war that they desperately wanted to enter reflected egregiously erroneous judgment on the part of Britain's American allies. Admiral William D. Leahy, the president's chief of staff, did not want the Soviets brought into the war, let alone paid to enter.[22]

However, if the Soviets desired to enter the war, they would have done so, assuming that the war did not end before they could prepare properly, whether or not the United States agreed to their price. Having entered, they surely would have taken something. The argument that Yalta bought moderation from the Soviets, who could have gone on in the absence of an agreement to take more, is specious. But there is some merit in Roosevelt's efforts to put together a package deal that he hoped would satisfy Soviet aspirations, while at the same time procure something in return.

President Roosevelt might have been justified in giving what he did to guarantee Stalin's support for Jiang, if he had secured a firm, definitive commitment on China, but he received no such commitment. The agreement stated that "the Soviet Union expresses its readiness to conclude with the National Government of China a pact of friendship and alliance between the USSR and China in order to render assistance to China with its armed forces for the purpose of liberating China from the Japanese yoke." This suggested that the Soviets were obliged to help the Chinese government only during the war against Japan. After the war was over they would be able to decide whether to continue to back the Nationalists or to throw their support to the Communists, depending on what suited their interests. Moreover, the words "readiness to conclude" gave the Soviets freedom to bargain with Jiang's government over the cost of the pact of friendship and alliance, and Stalin exacted a stiff price in negotiations during the summer of 1945.[23]

Totally apart from the criticism of the wisdom and morality of the agreement that surfaced in the United States, President Roosevelt's failure to secure a more precise pledge from Stalin allowed the Nationalist regime, and its friends in the United States, to place the obloquy of defeat by the Communists squarely on American policymakers. Not only did the Nationalists generally refuse to acknowledge their own responsibility for losing the mainland, but they also proceeded subsequently to make Yalta a central part of the sustaining ideology of Taiwan.[24]

Notes

[1]Hurley to Roosevelt, November 15, 1942, Patrick J. Hurley Papers, University of Oklahoma Library. See also Russell D. Buhite, *Patrick J. Hurley and American Foreign Policy*, p. 107.

[2]Herbert Feis, *Churchill-Roosevelt-Stalin: The War They Waged and the Peace They Sought*, pp. 403–04.

[3]Feis, *Churchill-Roosevelt-Stalin*, pp. 405–06.

[4]John L. Snell, *The Meaning of Yalta: Big Three Diplomacy and the New Balance of Power*, p. 134; John R. Deane, *The Strange Alliance: The Story of Our Efforts at Wartime Cooperation with Russia*, pp. 241–42, 246–47.

[5]Feis, *Churchill-Roosevelt-Stalin*, p. 466; *Foreign Relations: Yalta*, p. 378.

[6]*Foreign Relations: Yalta*, p. 650; Feis, *Churchill-Roosevelt-Stalin*, p. 501.

[7]*Foreign Relations: Yalta*, pp. 757–66.

[8]Ibid., pp. 834–36.

[9]Feis, *Churchill-Roosevelt-Stalin*, p. 503.

[10]*Foreign Relations: Yalta*, p. 766.

[11]Ibid., pp. 383, 383n (emphasis in original).

[12]Ibid., pp. 768–69. In addition to his concern about China, Roosevelt desired an independent Korea, which he thought he might jeopardize unless he brought the Soviets in as planned. See James Irving Matray, *The Reluctant Crusade: American Foreign Policy in Korea, 1941–1950*, p. 25.

[13]*Foreign Relations: Yalta*, p. 768.

[14]Ibid., p. 769.

[15]Ibid.

[16]Ibid., p. 771.

[17]Ibid., p. 984.

[18]Ibid., pp. 379–83.

[19]Ibid., pp. 385–88.

[20]Herbert Feis, *The China Tangle: The American Effort in China from Pearl Harbor to the Marshall Mission*, p. 251.

[21]Walter Millis, ed., *The Forrestal Diaries*, p. 55; memorandum by Charles E. Bohlen, May 28, 1945, U.S. Department of State, *Foreign Relations of the United States: Diplomatic Papers: The Conference of Berlin (The Potsdam Conference), 1945*, pp. 41–45. See also Russell D. Buhite, *Soviet-American Relations in Asia, 1945–1954*, pp. 103–06.

[22]See Snell, *The Meaning of Yalta*, p. 155. See also William D. Leahy, *I Was There: The Personal Story of the Chief of Staff to Presidents Roosevelt and Truman Based on His Notes and Diaries Made at the Time*; Anthony Eden, *The Eden Memoirs*, vol. 2, *The Reckoning*; and William H. Standley and Arthur A. Ageton, *Admiral Ambassador to Russia*, p. 499.

[23]Feis, *Churchill-Roosevelt-Stalin*, p. 516.

[24]Every school-age youngster in Taiwan learns that the "mistake" or "treachery" of Yalta is the main reason why the Nationalists fled the mainland. The government there has kept the myth alive, as have many of the island's scholars who deal with the World War II era and Sino-American relations.

VI
Iran, Yugoslavia, and the Declaration on Liberated Europe

The mixture of ideal principles and balance-of-power considerations that complicated discussions on some of the larger questions at Yalta also affected the conferees' ability to deal with less intrusive issues. That these matters did not generate the intense heat of the Polish or German negotiations does not mean that the sudden controversy arising from them would prove insignificant, either in the Crimean deliberations or in future U.S.-Soviet confrontations. A fair amount of controversy arose over Iran, for instance, as well as over Yugoslavia and the whole issue of the treatment of liberated European countries.

Iran became an object of contention at Yalta and in the months immediately preceding the conference because the Soviet Union reacted vigorously in the autumn of 1944 to efforts by British and U.S. oil companies to secure concessions in Iran. The Soviet response consisted of demands that the Iranian government in turn grant oil concessions to the Soviet Union in five northern provinces, demands that Iran resisted by suspending all petroleum negotiations until the end of the war. This exchange brought into sharp focus the conflicting interests of the three Allied powers, which throughout the war had shared in the occupation of Iran.

The problem began in 1941. In that year the Soviet Union, whose 1921 treaty with Iran specified that in case a third power threatened Russia it could send troops to Iran to help reduce the threat, began pressuring the Iranian government to expel German influence from the country. In mid-August the British joined the USSR in the representations but received little satisfaction from Shah Mohammed Reza Pahlavi, who was obviously impressed by the unchecked German successes in the war.

Consequently, on August 25, 1941, the British and Russians launched a coordinated attack on Iran, the Soviet Union driving in from the north and Great Britain from the south. On September 9 they imposed an agreement which placed Russia in control of the northern part of the country and Great Britain in control of much of the south and central regions. The British and Soviets agreed to withdraw their forces at the end of the war. Although not formally an occupying power, the United States in 1942, in order to ensure the continued flow of Lend-Lease materials to the Soviet Union, established a military mission in Iran. In 1943 it created the Persian Gulf Command, a noncombatant force of about 30,000 men which took over and operated Iran's railroads and principal highways. During the period of the American presence, the United States also furnished Iran with Lend-Lease goods.

Because American policymakers recognized that past and present attitudes on the part of the Soviet Union and Great Britain—Russia's desire for a warmwater port and Britain's strategic considerations in the Middle East and India—could make Iran a "danger point" in any postwar settlement, they began working on a policy to neutralize any potentially aggressive aspirations of the great powers. In January 1943, U.S. Foreign Service Officer John Jernegan drafted a memorandum, suggesting that the powers strengthen Iran, thus enabling it to stand independently, while at the same time pledging themselves to avoid taking advantage of Iranian weaknesses. Since the United States alone possessed the capability of giving aid, and would arouse less suspicion than either the British or Soviets in doing so, it should take the lead in guaranteeing Iran's prosperity, stability, and independence. Jernegan's memorandum advocated making Iran the "proving ground" for the Atlantic Charter.

The State Department endorsed the proving ground idea, and Secretary of State Cordell Hull pleaded for President Roosevelt's support. "If events are allowed to run their course unchecked," he stated, "it seems likely that either Russia or Great Britain, or both, will be led to take action which will seriously abridge, if not destroy, effective Iranian independence. That such action would be contrary to the principles of the Atlantic charter is obvious."[1] Hull feared that conflict over Iran would have worldwide repercussions, and Roosevelt agreed. The United States had a dual motive in its advocacy of principle: one was idealistic and the other eminently practical. Loss of Iran's independence would constitute a negation of the ideals for which the Allies claimed to be fighting, and such a negation "would destroy the confidence of the world in the good faith of the United Nations and would begin the disintegration of the peace structure which we hoped to set up."[2] More importantly, U.S. interest in oil development in Saudi Arabia could be jeopardized if a great power ensconced itself on the Iranian side of the Persian Gulf, where American firms were also interested in Iran.

Having formulated this policy, U.S. officials attempted at the Moscow Foreign Ministers' Conference to secure British and Soviet acceptance. The British had their own ideas about Iran and at Moscow suggested that all three occupying powers endorse a resolution agreeing to withdraw when the war ended. While such action did not conflict with basic American goals, Secretary Hull hesitated to approve the British declaration because he believed it necessary that U.S. forces, consisting in the main of engineering battalions, remain in the country until the Iranians themselves took over the railroads. Hull recommended that each country simply declare its withdrawal intentions unilaterally. At the same time, he favored a commitment to the principles worked out by the State Department. The Soviets on their part favored postponing any decision on withdrawal because of their unwillingness to discuss Iranian questions in the absence of an Iranian representative.

Failure of the Allies to work out a common policy at Moscow convinced Secretary Hull of the need to place Iran on the agenda at the Tehran Conference. At the beginning of that meeting, President Roosevelt asked his personal emissary Patrick Hurley to draft a declaration that might prove acceptable to all parties. Gathering up Jernegan's studies from within the Near Eastern Division of the State Department, as well as subsequent State Department pronouncements on the matter, Hurley worked out a brief statement which the three heads of state signed on December 1, 1943. Known as the Declaration on Iran, the statement acknowledged Iran's importance in the war effort and the hardship that the war imposed on it, pledged the Allies to cooperate in assisting Iran economically, and committed the three governments to maintain Iran's independence, sovereignty, and territorial integrity. Finally, the declaration endorsed the application in Iran of the Atlantic Charter principles.

American wartime planning for Iran's future did not end there. President Roosevelt encouraged Hurley to work out a further scheme to promote economic development in the country, a plan that foreshadowed the "Point Four" program of the late 1940s. It involved U.S. aid, adviser-experts, and the close scrutinizing of those corporations allowed to go into Iran, as well as the exportation of liberal-democratic principles.[3] Given this American agenda for Iran and the traditional British interests in preventing Soviet access to the Persian Gulf, it is little wonder that the events of 1944 would create concern. This is not to say that the two Western allies did not contribute to the problem; it is to argue, however, that the aggressive behavior of the Soviet Union precipitated it.

In early 1944 British and American oil companies began negotiations with the Iranian government to procure oil concessions in southern Iran. These were private commercial ventures, which both the London and U.S. embassies quickly became aware of but did not abet. Just as the negotiations seemed about to culminate successfully in September, a large contingent of Soviet officials, led by Deputy People's Commissar of Foreign Affairs S. I. Kavtaradze, appeared in Tehran and demanded a concession in northern Iran.[4] The Iranian government became justifiably alarmed as such a demand was too sweeping and general. It would grant a foreign government and not a private company large-scale, and possibly permanent, control over a sizable section of the country, and, unlike the British and American private companies, the Soviets made no offer to pay anything for their concession.

With the approval, if not actual encouragement, of London and Washington, Iran promptly announced that all oil negotiations would cease until the end of the war. Both the British and American governments offered perfunctory protestations at Iran's action and asked that British and U.S. companies receive equal treatment in any postwar concession granting. The Soviets, convinced that their Western allies had provoked the Iranian decision, reacted belligerently. They began a concerted and aggressive press attack on the Iranian government, a campaign so intense that it led to the resignation of Prime Minister Mohammed Saed.

Heated exchanges then occurred between the British and Americans on one side and the Soviets on the other. Calling attention to the Declaration on Iran, the U.S. embassy in Moscow on November 1, 1944 urged the Soviets to respect the sovereignty and territorial integrity of Iran. In a lengthy and defiant reply of December 28, 1944, the Soviet leaders accused the Iranians of "disloyal" and unfriendly action, indicated that their demand for a concession would not violate the Declaration on Iran, and accused the American government of an unsympathetic attitude toward the Soviet Union.[5] The British, willing as they were to make some allowances for Soviet aspirations in Eastern Europe, expressed no similar sympathy on Middle Eastern questions. As Prime Minister Churchill put it in a message of mid-January to President Roosevelt, "If the Russians are now able not only to save their face by securing the fall of the Persian Prime Minister who opposed them, but also to secure what they want by their use of the big stick, Persia is not the only place where the bad effect will be felt."[6] Churchill strongly believed that the Western allies should secure a favorable resolution of the Iranian issue at the Yalta meetings.

British Foreign Minister Anthony Eden first brought up the matter during the Crimean sessions at a meeting of the foreign ministers on February 8. Averring that the Iranians should be masters in their own house, he urged that the Allies avoid interference in Iran's internal affairs. To this end, and to avoid conflict among the Allies, he suggested that the three governments indicate their willingness to withdraw as soon as the supply routes were closed, which was earlier than required by the Tehran declaration. In the meantime, the Allies should not press further for oil concessions until their troops were all withdrawn.[7] In urging this action, Eden advised that he was not disputing the Soviets' claim nor disparaging their motives. In fact, the British would not object to Russian acquisition of oil in northern Iran since the Soviet Union constituted a natural market for it.

Molotov's reply demonstrated Soviet sensitivity. He did not want to discuss early troop withdrawal since, as he expressed it, this was a new question never "placed before the Soviet Government until today." To consider early withdrawal would mean amending the treaty that Iran had signed with the British and Soviets of January 29, 1942; this would take time for study. He then launched into a defense of his country's oil negotiations. At first the Iranians were favorable toward a Soviet oil concession, apparently recognizing the mutual interests served by such a concession and the consistency of the Soviet request with the Declaration on Iran. Then, Molotov said, the Iranian position changed to one of permitting no negotiations until the end of

the war. What the Soviets had attempted to do in sending Kavtaradze to Tehran was to persuade the Iranian leadership to
go back to its earlier position, implying that, since the Western allies had convinced the Iranian government to move from
the first position to the second, it was perfectly logical to expect
the Soviets to convince them to move back to the first.[8]

Secretary of State Stettinius supported Eden. He expressed
sympathy with the proposal for an early withdrawal of troops.
On the matter of oil concessions, American firms, he noted, were
in the same situation as the Soviets in that their negotiations for
concessions also were put in abeyance until war's end. Concerned
about Soviet sensitivity, both Stettinius and Eden repeatedly told
Molotov that they had no objections to Soviet acquisition of
Iranian oil at the proper time.[9]

In order to avoid any sort of agreement that would prevent
Soviet freedom of action, Molotov suggested limiting action to
an "exchange of views" on the subject and having Kavtaradze
come to the conference to make a report. This would effectively
put the issue to rest, given that the Crimean Conference was
nearly over. Neither Eden nor Stettinius was willing to accept
Molotov's reasoning. They raised the matter on February 9, again
urging a pledge to withdraw troops as soon as the supply routes
were closed. On February 10, Eden, with Stettinius's approval,
attempted to gain the Soviet foreign minister's acceptance of
either a communiqué on Iran, or a statement of reaffirmation
of the Declaration on Iran. Molotov refused to budge.[10]

Apart from raising the level of frustration among the Western
allies, Eden's insistence on discussing Iran had little impact. Not
only did Molotov prove intransigent but also talking with Stalin
did little good. The latter seemed more agreeable, telling Eden
"never talk to Molotov about Iran. . . . He is very sore with Iran.
If you want to talk about it, talk to me."[11] Stalin, however, had
taken no action on the proposal for an announcement to remove
troops when the conferees left Yalta. Iran became a postwar
problem, and the focal point of crisis in the spring of 1946 when
the Soviets not only refused to withdraw but also seemed ready
to dominate the country. It took vigorous steps by the United
States, acting through the United Nations, to secure the removal
of Soviet forces.

Although it involved the United States only tangentially, the
Allies became embroiled in controversy over Yugoslavia as well,
in particular over a proposal by Prime Minister Churchill to

amend an existing agreement between Josip Broz Tito, Yugoslav partisan leader, and Ivan Subasić, prime minister representing the exile government in London. This was a conflict with a four-year history that is better comprehended if examined against the background of the war itself.

As in Poland, the Western allies hoped to preserve a measure of influence in Yugoslavia, while promoting governmental unity, the belief being that civil strife would lead to a proxy struggle among Western-oriented forces and those that would find support from the Soviet Union. The Soviets on their part desired the increased influence—optimally, a foothold on the Adriatic—that they hoped would come with the success of Tito's partisans. Within Yugoslavia the wartime division of power involved forces, under the direction of Tito, that often found themselves at odds with those under nominal control, or at least in part directed by the exile government.

By the time the Germans invaded Yugoslavia in April 1941, King Peter II and his government had fled first to Jerusalem and then to London. Although the king tried to maintain contact with resistance movements within his country, his control over them remained tenuous at best. Late in 1941, upon hearing of the heroic deeds of General Draža Mihajlović, King Peter sought to coopt him and in January 1942 appointed him minister of war. The British endorsed this move and joined in the support of Mihajlović, providing his forces with weapons, medical supplies, and other essential materials, as well as military advisers who were parachuted in. Because of severe repression at the hands of the Germans and the collaborationist activities of some of Mihajlović's officers, not to mention critical shortages in supplies, his group was soon superseded by other resistance forces. British confidence in Mihajlović gradually diminished.[12]

In 1943 the British for two reasons began to support Tito's partisans as well as the followers of the London Yugoslavs. Churchill wanted to inflict as many casualties as possible on German forces in the Balkans, and he hoped, once the battle for Italy had turned in the Allies' favor, to solicit American concurrence to land in Yugoslavia. From there Allied forces would push northward into Austria and Germany.

Having committed themselves to aid both resistance groups, the British also tried to promote cooperation between the two and sought to enlist the support of the Soviet Union in their endeavor. This seemed the best way to preserve the position of the government in exile and to give the Yugoslavs a chance at future self-government. Furthermore, it seemed necessary if the British were to prevent Communist domination of the country, a likely prospect if civil conflict proceeded to its logical conclusion. For a while, in the fall of 1943, the Soviets adopted a friendly attitude toward King Peter's government—perhaps because Stalin found Marshal Tito too independent and uncontrollable—and indicated some support for the British proposal.

In mid-June of 1944 the British pressured the exile government into a reorganization, resulting in the elevation of Subasić to prime minister. At the instigation of the British, he then concluded an agreement with Tito in which he recognized the marshal's temporary administration. Tito accepted, at least until the end of the war, the continuation of the monarchy.[13]

Amid reports that Communist successes within the country were moving Yugoslavia toward the East, Churchill and Tito met in August 1944 at Caserta to discuss both military and political questions. The British prime minister asked for Tito's cooperation in an Allied landing on the Adriatic coast of Yugoslavia, a request that Tito acceded to with alacrity, even to the point of agreeing to have his partisans open a small port for Allied use. He also consented to talk with Subasić, at which meeting the two men decided to unite all Yugoslav naval forces. All this, however, did not mean that Tito had accepted the British program.

By fall 1944, as Russian forces moved into eastern Yugoslavia, Tito began to adjust his relations with the British, partially to accommodate the Soviet Union but mostly to guarantee his own control over the country. Without informing British officers stationed at his headquarters, he flew off to Moscow in September to confer with Stalin and to secure Soviet aid in expelling the Germans. Because Tito was seeking power and did not want to share it, during these discussions he vigorously resisted Stalin's advice that he allow King Peter to return, and he informed the Soviet leader that his offer of cooperation with an Allied landing on the Adriatic coast was no longer valid. Tito's partisans would put up stiff military resistance against any such move.

Meanwhile, Churchill and Stalin had divided their responsibilities for Yugoslavia. In their famous meeting of October 9 in Moscow, the two Allied leaders had settled on a sphere-of-influence agreement put forward by Churchill in which, among other things, the Soviet Union was to have 90 percent influence in Romania, the British 90 percent in Greece, and the two nations each would have 50 percent in Yugoslavia. Having thus agreed to work together in the Balkans, Churchill and Stalin had no major trouble between themselves regarding Yugoslavia prior to Yalta. However, as is frequently the case in sphere-of-influence arrangements, it is much easier for major powers to agree than to convince competing indigenous forces to cooperate. Tito's power within the country made it virtually impossible for the government in exile to gain an equal footing with him, thereby signaling that the British would have difficulty influencing events there.

Tito and Subasić concluded an agreement on December 7 which both the British and Americans considered unsatisfactory. Envisioning the creation of an eventual unified government, the two Yugoslavs agreed that given Tito's strength his group would have the dominating position of the executive offices and in the anti-Fascist Council of National Liberation, which would have legislative power until three months after total liberation, when national elections would be held to elect a new constituent assembly. Meanwhile, King Peter would not return unless the people requested it. As the British quickly realized, there was little here for the exile government. The U.S. State Department also understood. "Stripped of its generalities," Secretary Stettinius wrote, "the agreement provides for a thoroughgoing recording of administrative, legislative, electoral and institutional procedures, in which one group, even though it may be the strongest in the country, would have practically complete and exclusive power."[14]

Although the British did not fully approve of the Tito-Subasić accord, they decided to support it as the best arrangement possible under the circumstances. Consequently, they sought, without success, to draw the United States into the policy. British support, however, did not persuade King Peter that he should acquiesce, despite Subasić's strong recommendation, and for a while the king threatened to overturn the agreement. Only strong pressure from Churchill in late January 1945 convinced him to dispatch Subasić to carry it out. This was the situation when the Yalta Conference convened.

At Yalta, Churchill and Eden, in an attempt to make it more democratic, proposed two amendments to the Tito-Subasić accord. One would have allowed noncollaborationists from the former Yugoslav parliament to participate in the new legislative body. The other would have made this legislative body subject to the approval of the constituent assembly, which was scheduled to come into existence after the entire country was liberated. Stalin, fearful of a British attempt to undercut Tito, and because he saw potential advantage in proceeding with the agreement as written, refused to accept any amendments. As a result, there were no meaningful changes made. Just before the Crimean Conference adjourned, Churchill and Stalin agreed to send messages to Tito and Subasić, urging the early implementation of the December 7 accord. Then, after a new government based on this accord had come into existence, it would announce its intention to accede to the spirit of the two amendments. This "compromise," which President Roosevelt joined in endorsing, meant that Tito could effectively do as he pleased.[15]

In the case of Yugoslavia, Great Britain equated British influence with the acceptance of liberal-democratic procedures. Unfortunately, Tito and his partisans had the upper hand militarily and therefore politically; he, in effect, had made a revolution during the war. Interestingly, Tito might very well have retained power under the democratic processes that Churchill and his American ally so vigorously espoused. In any event, that the ideals put forward by the U.S. government for dealing with liberated countries had no chance of acceptance in Yugoslavia was apparent well before Yalta.

Allied treatment of territory liberated from German control was a matter that had long troubled American policymakers. As early as the 1943 Moscow Foreign Ministers' Conference, Secretary Hull had recommended making a tripartite Allied announcement on liberated areas which would enunciate democratic principles. The foreign ministers, however, could not agree on how to word it and promptly relegated the issue to the newly created European Advisory Commission. Nothing came from that body either. By the time the United States advanced the idea at Yalta, it was too late to have meaning in any area liberated by the Soviet army.

A threefold concern motivated U.S. policymakers to introduce the declaration. First, since in the American psyche the war against Germany and Japan had become a crusade in pursuit of transcendent moral values, one of which was representative self-government, it followed that the United States should promote the cause of democracy in liberated countries. The advancing Red Army made it highly problematic that representative democracy would have any chance unless the Soviets joined in a pledge to promote it. Second, a rift had developed between the Soviets and the British despite their October 1944 sphere-of-influence arrangement. The British were convinced that the Soviets planned to impose Communist governments as far as their armies reached, while the Soviets believed that the British desired to erect a cordon sanitaire on the Russian border. Such differences could destroy the alliance and preclude postwar cooperation. A collateral and third concern was that, if the American people got the impression that the war promoted unilateral territorial and political aggrandizement, which a new world organization would underwrite, they would reject the UN concept.[16]

Neither the Soviets nor the British were as enthusiastic as the Americans about the Declaration on Liberated Europe, although the British warmly endorsed the provisions as long as they did not apply the Atlantic Charter to the British Empire.[17] The Soviets had no intention of observing it no matter what the Big Three decided at Yalta. Indeed, Stalin first sought to use some of the declaration's language to his advantage. Then, hoping to weaken its impact, Molotov offered amendments. Stalin liked the part of the declaration that said the Allies would eradicate "Nazism and Fascism" because such a policy would allow the Soviets to label as "Fascist" and disqualify from public life all those elements in Poland that were not subservient to the Soviet Union.[18] This became clear during discussions on Poland at the sixth plenary meeting of February 9. Molotov's first amendment proposed that the Allies lend support "to the political leaders of those countries who have taken an active part in the struggle against the German invaders," an amendment patently designed to give special position to Communist elements in the liberated countries and to allow the Soviets to make distinctions in their practice of "representative" democracy.[19] Stalin sarcastically added that the amendment would not apply to Greece, where the British had suppressed the Communists. Roosevelt and Churchill were not willing to accept Molotov's proposal and remanded it to the foreign ministers.

Stettinius and Eden remonstrated strenuously against Molotov's amendment at the foreign ministers' meeting later on the 9th. Stettinius indicated that in the United States it would not be acceptable for domestic political reasons but, more importantly, it would require unwarranted and continuous intrusion of the Allied powers into the internal affairs of the liberated countries.[20] When it became obvious to Molotov during this meeting and one the following day that he could not secure acceptance of this amendment, he came forward with a second one. Again his intention was to guarantee freedom of action for the Soviet Union by preventing the accession to power in Eastern Europe of a government not controllable by the Soviets. This time Molotov suggested that the language of the penultimate paragraph of the declaration be changed. As introduced by the United States it read: "When, in the opinion of the three governments, conditions in any European liberated state or any former Axis satellite state in Europe make such action necessary, they will immediately establish appropriate machinery for the carrying out of the joint responsibilities set forth in this declaration." The Soviets, seeing this statement as troublesome, proposed that the paragraph be worded: "They will take measures for the carrying out of mutual consultation." Molotov wanted only consultation, not action.[21]

Despite the arguments of Churchill and Eden on February 10 that mutual consultation was meaningless and weakened the declaration, the Big Three finally approved a version similar to Molotov's phrasing. Eden came forward with language acceptable to Stalin that may have made the British delegation feel better but was equally vague and useless.

As finally approved the document read as follows:

> The Premier of the Union of Soviet Socialist Republics, the Prime Minister of the United Kingdom, and the President of the United States of America have consulted with each other in the common interests of the peoples of their countries and those of liberated Europe. They jointly declare their mutual agreement to concert during the temporary period of instability in liberated Europe the policies of their three governments in assisting the peoples liberated from the domination of Nazi Germany and the peoples of the former Axis satellite states of Europe to solve by democratic means their pressing political and economic problems.
>
> The establishment of order in Europe and the rebuilding of national economic life must be achieved by processes which will enable the liberated peoples to destroy the last vestiges of Nazism and Fascism and to creat[e] democratic institutions of their own choice. This is a principle of the Atlantic Charter—the right of all peoples to choose the form of government under which they will live—the restoration of sovereign rights and self-government to those peoples who have been forcibly deprived of them by the aggressor nations.

To foster the conditions in which the liberated peoples may exercise these rights, the three governments will jointly assist the people in any European liberated state or former Axis satellite state in Europe where in their judgment conditions require (a) to establish conditions of internal peace; (b) to carry out emergency measures for the relief of distressed people; (c) to form interim governmental authorities broadly representative of all democratic elements in the population and pledged to the earliest possible establishment through free elections of governments responsive to the will of the people; and (d) to facilitate where necessary the holding of such elections.

The three governments will consult the other United Nations and provisional authorities or other governments in Europe when matters of direct interest to them are under consideration.

When, in the opinion of the three governments, conditions in any European liberated state or any former Axis satellite state in Europe make such action necessary, *they will immediately consult together on the measures necessary to discharge the joint responsibilities set forth in this declaration.*

By this declaration we reaffirm our faith in the principles of the Atlantic Charter, our pledge in the Declaration by the United Nations, and our determination to build in cooperation with other peace-loving nations a world order under law, dedicated to peace, security, freedom and the general well-being of all mankind.[22]

With the provision for consultation—that is, unanimous consent before enforcement measures were contemplated—the Soviets must have seen the declaration as nothing more than empty rhetoric and of no danger to their interests. How President Roosevelt perceived the declaration is unclear, but he must have viewed it as little more than a lofty expression of American principles. The president was not committed to enforcement machinery, as he demonstrated in his refusal to support Secretary Stettinius's proposal for a High Commission on Liberated Europe. Further, two weeks after Yalta he greeted, with considerable indifference, Stalin's brutal ultimatum to the government of Romania that, unless the Communists obtained power shortly, Russia would "not be responsible for the continuance of Rumania as an independent state." Moreover, Roosevelt was willing, even while applying these principles to Eastern Europe, to violate them in his deal with Stalin on Northeast Asia.[23]

The Declaration on Liberated Europe in sum did not occupy much time at Yalta, nor was its approval an important consequence of the conference. By the time the conference convened, the Soviet Union held such a dominant military position in Eastern Europe that a Soviet sphere of influence there seemed predetermined. Given these circumstances, the declaration may be interpreted as little more than an attempt, in the face of reality, to keep American aspirations alive while satisfying domestic political requirements.

Notes

[1]*Foreign Relations, 1943*, 4:377–78.

[2]Ibid., pp. 386–88. See also Bruce Kuniholm, *The Origins of the Cold War in the Near East: Great Power Conflict and Diplomacy in Iran, Turkey, and Greece*, pp. 130–208.

[3]*Foreign Relations, 1943*, 4:413–14, 417–19.

[4]*Foreign Relations: Yalta*, p. 342.

[5]Ibid., p. 343.

[6]Ibid., p. 337.

[7]Ibid., pp. 738–39.

[8]Ibid., pp. 739–40.

[9]Ibid., p. 740. See also Kuniholm, *Origins of the Cold War*, pp. 214–16.

[10]Ibid., pp. 740, 877.

[11]Anthony Eden, *The Eden Memoirs*, vol. 2, *The Reckoning*, p. 596.

[12]Herbert Feis, *Churchill-Roosevelt-Stalin: The War They Waged and the Peace They Sought*, pp. 201–02.

[13]Ibid., p. 422.

[14]*Foreign Relations: Yalta*, pp. 250–53, 256; Feis, *Churchill-Roosevelt-Stalin*, p. 543.

[15]Ibid., pp. 919–20; Feis, *Churchill-Roosevelt-Stalin*, pp. 544–45.

[16]Feis, *Churchill-Roosevelt-Stalin*, p. 549.

[17]*Foreign Relations: Yalta*, p. 848.

[18]Diane S. Clemens, *Yalta*, p. 205.

[19]*Foreign Relations: Yalta*, p. 848.

[20]Ibid., p. 868.

[21]Ibid. See also Clemens, *Yalta*, p. 264.

[22]*Foreign Relations: Yalta*, p. 972 (author's emphasis).

[23]James F. Byrnes, *Speaking Frankly*, p. 53; John Lewis Gaddis, *Russia, the Soviet Union, and the United States: An Interpretive History*, pp. 163–64; Walter LaFeber, *America, Russia, and the Cold War, 1945–1966*, p. 17.

VII
Yalta and the
Palestine Problem

On the evening before the Yalta Conference was scheduled to
end, President Roosevelt told Winston Churchill of his planned
itinerary for the trip home: he would stop in Egypt at the Great
Bitter Lake for conferences with King Farouk of Egypt, King
Ibn Saud of Saudi Arabia, and Emperor Haile Selassie of Ethiopia. According to Harry Hopkins, Churchill was "flabbergasted"
at the news and later came to him in a "greatly disturbed" frame
of mind to find out what was happening. Unless reassured,
Churchill announced that he would have to go see the Middle
Eastern sovereigns himself, the implication being that he was
worried that the president's visit would undercut British influence in the Middle East. Hopkins's response to the prime minister is interesting in that he said he did not know what Roosevelt
was doing, but his guess was that "it was a lot of horseplay," in
which the president would enjoy the "colorful panoply" of oriental potentates coming to him.[1]

With regard to Hopkins's recounting of this affair, three facts
are important to mention. That Churchill was flabbergasted at
the news is false since he and Roosevelt had discussed the matter
at Malta, that Churchill was worried about the president's trip
is unclear, and that certainly Hopkins's judgment that it was
just horseplay was uninformed.[2]

President Roosevelt's egress from Yalta began on February 11.
After the ceremonial dinner and the exchange of gifts among the
Allies, Roosevelt was lifted into his Packard limousine for the
drive along the rocky coast near Yalta and then north to Balaklava, the first stop on his overland trip across the Crimean peninsula. Averell Harriman and his daughter shared the president's
car. From Balaklava, important in history as the site of the charge
of the Light Brigade nearly a century earlier, Roosevelt's party
moved north through Sevastopol to the coast and finally to the

supply ship *Catoctin*, where the president would spend the night. On February 12, Roosevelt prepared for the next leg of his journey, which would take him ultimately to the airfield at Saki. Because it was impossible to go by the direct mountain road, given the danger of rock slides, the president would have to travel to Simferopol and then on to Saki, a circuitous route of more than seventy miles. This trip took three and one-half hours and was followed by a ceremony in which the president reviewed an honor guard of Soviet troops. At Saki, Roosevelt boarded a C-54 aircraft for the flight to Egypt.

Again, because of Roosevelt's cardiovascular condition, his plane had to fly a long distance at low altitude, and his flight was exceedingly difficult. The distance was slightly over 1,000 miles, which the plane would cover in a tortuous five hours at 9,000 feet. Escorted by U.S. fighter planes, which joined the flight pattern off the coast of Lebanon, the president's C-54 and two other four-engine planes flew on a course across the Black Sea, then over Turkish territory near Ankara, and on to the Mediterranean.

The president landed at Deversoir, an American military airfield near Ismailia, Egypt, in late afternoon on February 12 several hours before the communiqués on Yalta were to be released in the Allied capitals. A contingent of air force officers and S. Pinkney Tuck, the U.S. minister to Egypt, greeted Roosevelt with appropriate honors prior to his transfer to the cruiser *Quincy*, which lay at anchor in the Great Bitter Lake. There the president would await the arrival of the three sovereigns.[3]

King Farouk, a portly young man of twenty-five years, accompanied by his aides and the U.S. minister, was the first to arrive on February 13. Roosevelt greeted him on the deck of the *Quincy* behind a gun mount. Everyone present waited anxiously to find out the reason for the president's visit, not least King Farouk himself, who seemed puzzled by the whole affair. Roosevelt's remarks did not help much. Egyptian-American trade would assume great importance in the future, he said, especially the trade in long staple cotton, which he hoped the Egyptians would grow in greater abundance. Moreover, Egypt could expect a large postwar influx of American tourists who would want to indulge their curiosity about the Pyramids and the Nile River. Then Roosevelt told Farouk what a wonderful people the Egyptians were and how he admired their grand history. After about one hour of such pleasantries and innocuous banter, the party adjourned for lunch, following which the president directed his aides to take the king on a tour of the *Quincy*. Having discussed nothing of much substance or consequence, Roosevelt dismissed the king at 3:30 P.M., after giving him a copy of his presidential inaugural address and, more impressive to the king, a twin-engine C-47.

Haile Selassie was next, arriving at 5:30. Flown in from Addis Ababa by the American minister, the emperor, a wooly-headed, bearded, dark-eyed, diminutive man of five feet three inches, understood no more about the purpose of Roosevelt's visit than did the Egyptian king, nor did the president's remarks prove edifying to him. Roosevelt allowed that the airplane put Ethiopia in closer contact with the rest of the world, and he thanked the emperor for American legation property in Addis Ababa but said nothing of significance. All political issues introduced during the conversation were initiated by the emperor, including his desire for a port and arms assistance. Roosevelt made no commitments of any sort.[4] Apparently concerned that all Middle Eastern potentates receive roughly equal treatment, the president also dispatched his Ethiopian guest on a tour of the *Quincy*. After an exchange of gifts, in which Roosevelt gave Haile Selassie four American automobiles, the latter took his leave at 7:00 o'clock, the total visit lasting barely ninety minutes.

King Ibn Saud arrived the next day on board the U.S. destroyer *Murphy*, which had been dispatched to Jidda several days before to fetch him. Nearly disabled by age, obesity, and arthritis, the king had been loaded aboard by pulling him up in a whaleboat, and he had been kept relatively tranquil during the trip by the U.S. officers' indulgence of his cultural idiosyncrasies. The Americans set up a tent on deck where the king and his aides could eat and pray, made space for the dozen or so live sheep that would be slaughtered for the sustenance of the king's party, and tried to provide regular "entertainment." When the king and his attendants, consisting of nine slaves, a physician, an astrologer, an official food taster, and a bevy of assistants, grew bored, the men of the *Murphy* would fire the big guns and drop depth charges; Ibn Saud, after all, was a warrior.

When the *Murphy* finally delivered the king to the *Quincy* on the 14th, the sight Roosevelt and his subordinates beheld must have raised questions about the wisdom of the president's mission. Certainly it brought scornful amusement.[5] On deck the berobed king sat on a gold chair in front of the flapping tent.

To his right and left were rich oriental rugs. Scattered about were dried sheep guts, blood spatterings from the slaughter of the animals, several live sheep milling about, and one dead one hanging from the jack staff.[6]

Ibn Saud was quickly lifted from the destroyer to the *Quincy* for the start of his conversations with Roosevelt, the most substantive of all the talks during the president's mission to the Great Bitter Lake. After a brief exchange on deck, in which the king suggested that he and the president were "twins," both in age and infirmities, and expressed admiration for Roosevelt's wheelchair (Roosevelt gave the king his backup chair but it proved too small), the two heads of state got down to business. The main topic was Zionism, the issue that initially had motivated the president's Middle Eastern detour.[7]

Roosevelt introduced the subject, asking Ibn Saud for his advice about Jewish refugees driven from their homes in Europe. The king animatedly responded that the Jews should return "to live in the lands from which they were driven." If it were impossible for them to return to their homelands, they should be settled on space provided them in the Axis countries. Whether or not this seemed sensible to Roosevelt, he smiled and opined agreeably that a great many could go to Poland. "The Germans," he pointed out, "appear to have killed three million Polish Jews, by which count there should be space in Poland for the resettlement of many homeless Jews."[8]

Ibn Saud, as he had done many times before, made himself perfectly clear that he held no brief for Zionism, and under no circumstances would he condone the settlement of Jews in Palestine. Legitimate Arab rights in their own lands were under attack, leading him to the belief that the Jews and Arabs could not cooperate in Palestine or any other country. Continued Jewish immigration and land purchases constituted a serious threat to the Arabs who would resist the intrusion. "Arabs," he warned, "would choose to die rather than yield their lands to the Jews."[9] Having unburdened himself so forcefully, the king then asked Roosevelt for American understanding and assistance. Roosevelt quickly promised his support, acknowledging that he "would do nothing to assist the Jews against the Arabs and would make no move hostile to the Arab people."[10] This did not mean, he hastened to add, that there would not be a lot of pro-Zionist rhetoric within the United States, statements that he could not control.

Searching for a means to mollify his Arab guest and perhaps make him more amenable to Jewish immigration, the president went on to suggest ways to make the desert bloom. Once a farmer himself, Roosevelt was interested in promoting irrigation, tree planting, and the development of waterpower. Increased cultivation of the desert would "provide living for a greater population of Arabs." Saud did not buy this proposal. He thanked the president for promoting agriculture, but admitted he was not enthusiastic about his country's agricultural and public works development "if this prosperity would be inherited by the Jews."[11]

If Roosevelt hoped that through personal diplomacy with the Middle Eastern sovereigns, especially Ibn Saud, he could find a formula for avoiding the domestic dilemma over the Palestine issue, he must have been sorely disappointed. In any event, that was his intention at the Great Bitter Lake conferences. Hopkins was wrong about the trip. Roosevelt was anxious to return to Washington. The visit was difficult and time consuming, and he would enjoy the "horseplay" only if it had its serious side benefits. It seems apparent that this Middle Eastern mission is best understood in context of the Palestine problem and the president's attempt and failure at Yalta to find any glimmer of cooperation from his allies in resolving it.

Roosevelt was in a bind over Palestine, a predicament that extended back several years but became more immediate with the 1944 election. Throughout the first four years of the European war, the United States at least tacitly supported the British White Paper of 1939 on Palestine, which pledged the creation of an independent Palestinian state with an Arab majority. In 1943 this seemed particularly wise, given the apparent need to court Arab goodwill in the search for adequate oil supplies. President Roosevelt, however, in the meantime, became personally sympathetic with the Zionist cause and by 1944 began to recognize the political benefits in taking a publicly pro-Zionist position. Public opinion in the United States, fed by an aggressive American Zionist pressure group, became strongly in favor of the idea of a refuge for Jews in Palestine.

The Democratic party platform in 1944 contained a plank supporting "the opening of Palestine to unrestricted Jewish immigration," and President Roosevelt strongly endorsed the plank. He sent a letter in October to the American Zionists' Conference stating that "I know how long and how ardently the

Jewish people have worked and prayed for the establishment of Palestine as a Jewish Commonwealth, and if reelected I shall help to bring about its realization."[12] How to retain good relations with Arab leaders, while adopting such blatantly pro-Zionist positions, became a compelling requirement for U.S. officials.

In lieu of a better plan, which could come later, Roosevelt and his advisers followed a ploy during the war which involved public statements and secret assurances. To satisfy the Zionists, the president would issue strongly worded pronouncements favoring their cause; to pacify the Arabs, he would issue private assurances that the pro-Zionist statements were nothing more than political blather. He would further assure the Arabs that the United States would not alter its position on Palestine without first consulting Arab leaders.[13]

The public-private ploy was useful temporarily, and Roosevelt was obviously still employing it at the Great Bitter Lake meeting with Ibn Saud, but it eventually had to be replaced with something more concrete that would accommodate the interests of both Arabs and Jews and prevent a future Middle Eastern crisis. Roosevelt thought trusteeship might be the answer, an arrangement that would make Palestine a Holy Land for all three religions, and he passed the idea along to the State Department for study.[14]

Accordingly, the Near Eastern Division of the State Department and other planners for the postwar period went to work in an endeavor to craft a detailed plan. What they came up with, and what the president took with him to Yalta, was a scheme to internationalize Palestine. Great Britain would act as trustee over Palestine, which would be declared an international trusteeship. A board of overseers from the Christian, Moslem, and Jewish communities of the world would serve as advisers to the British, and the trustee power would determine the extent of Jewish immigration. Land would be divided between Arabs and Jews, with each responsible for land sales in their respective area.[15]

Roosevelt hoped to secure a thorough airing of the Palestine problem during the Crimean sessions, as well as a formula for its solution, but nothing of the sort took place. Churchill, who believed Palestine to be a British prerogative and who did not want to reveal a British cabinet plan to partition the area, put the damper on with a negative response when the president brought up the matter at Malta on February 2. The prime minister did not wish to discuss Palestine at Yalta, although he indicated no objection to Roosevelt arranging, after the Crimean meetings, a conference with Middle Eastern leaders on board the *Quincy*. Except for a brief mention on the day before the conference ended when Stalin asked Roosevelt if he intended to make concessions to Ibn Saud, the Palestine issue did not arise at Yalta. The president told Stalin that he intended to discuss the "entire Palestine question" with the king.[16]

Recognizing that his chances to achieve a formula at Yalta were virtually nonexistent, Roosevelt decided, immediately after his talk with Churchill at Malta, to arrange the Middle Eastern trip. If no sign of a way out of the Palestine dilemma presented itself during the Middle East visits, at least the president could fall back on the ploy of giving private assurances to the Arabs. This was the reason for his comments to Ibn Saud on February 14.

In keeping with prior use of the ploy, and consistent with his own disposition in handling such controversial issues, the president chose, upon returning to the United States, to reiterate his support for Zionism. Moreover, in comments to Jewish leaders, he created the impression that he and Prime Minister Churchill, and perhaps Stalin, had reached an accord to the effect that Palestine would be given over to the Jews.[17]

The foregoing account is not intended to imply that Palestine was a burning issue in the minds of any of the Allied leaders at the time of the Yalta Conference; they had far more pressing matters to occupy their thoughts. Nor is the account any more than a sketchy explication of the Palestine problem as it existed in the final months of the war. It is necessary to address the issue, however, to explain why the president of the United States, so frail of health and so pressed for time, would undertake such a costly and demanding detour on his return from the Crimea.

Having concluded his conversations with Ibn Saud, Roosevelt prepared for a final round of talks with some of his advisers and with Churchill before setting his course for home. The *Quincy* sailed for Alexandria in late afternoon of the 14th, arriving at the ancient Egyptian city the next morning. There Roosevelt met briefly with Secretary Stettinius, Ambassador to Great Britain John Winant, Soviet expert Charles Bohlen, and Assistant Secretary of State H. Freeman Matthews to talk in general terms about the Yalta accords. Churchill boarded the *Quincy* just before

1:00 P.M. and stayed until 4:00 o'clock, but much of the time was devoted to an extended luncheon in which the president's daughter and Churchill's son and daughter participated. The substantive conversations were therefore limited. However, the two Allied leaders did discuss the military situation in the Far East.

After leaving Alexandria the president's trip was marked by hard work, disappointment, and sorrow. Scheduled to present an address to Congress soon after his arrival in the United States, Roosevelt expected Hopkins, his longtime assistant, to help in its drafting. Hopkins, who had been ill for months and who had spent much of his time at Yalta confined to his bed, refused to return home on the *Quincy*. He insisted that he would leave the ship at Algiers and arrange to rest for several days at Marrakech before flying to Washington. Roosevelt became very angry at this desertion, which forced him to summon from London Samuel I. Rosenman, who had not been present at Yalta, to help him prepare his speech.[18] It also forced the president to become more actively involved in the writing of his address, and at this stage he was less fit physically than Hopkins. Furthermore, Roosevelt suffered a devastating emotional blow on his return trip when General Edwin M. Watson, his military aide for twelve years and secretary for five, died of a cerebral hemorrhage two days after the *Quincy* left Algiers.

After ten days in the Atlantic, Roosevelt and his party finally docked at Newport News on the evening of February 27 and then took the presidential train to Washington, arriving the next morning. The round-trip to Yalta had taken almost five weeks, during which the president had traveled in excess of 13,800 miles. All who saw him or worked with him came to the similar conclusion that he was a dying man who must have felt the strain of such a long, physically, and mentally taxing voyage. Lord Charles Moran, Churchill's physician, who saw Roosevelt at Yalta, put it most succinctly: "He has all the symptoms of hardening of the arteries of the brain in an advanced stage, so that I give him only a few months to live."[19] Assuming that Roosevelt's death was imminent whether or not he had traveled halfway around the world to meet his allies, and discounting the difficulty of the trip, a number of questions remain, questions that would arise even if the summit conference had been held in Washington.

Notes

[1]Memorandum by Hopkins, Harry L. Hopkins Papers, Box 337, Folder 21, Franklin D. Roosevelt Library.

[2]Both Admiral Leahy and Secretary of State Stettinius reported overhearing the prime minister and the president discuss at Malta the meeting with the Middle Eastern leaders. See William D. Leahy, *I Was There: The Personal Story of the Chief of Staff to Presidents Roosevelt and Truman Based on His Notes and Diaries Made at the Time*, p. 295; and Edward R. Stettinius, Jr., *Roosevelt and the Russians: The Yalta Conference*, p. 72.

[3]See Jim Bishop, *FDR's Last Year: April 1944–April 1945*, pp. 394–408, for a lively account of Roosevelt's egress from Yalta and arrival at the Great Bitter Lake.

[4]See *Foreign Relations, 1945*, 8:6.

[5]The summary of the king's interests provided to Roosevelt prior to his Middle Eastern visit stated that "in his pleasures the king follows the pattern of his Prophet in preferring women, prayer, and perfume." Franklin D. Roosevelt Papers, n.d., Map Room File, Box 165, Folder 9.

[6]See William Eddy, *F.D.R. Meets Ibn Saud*. See also Michael F. Reilly, *Reilly of the White House*.

[7]*Foreign Relations, 1945*, 8:7.

[8]Ibid., p. 2.

[9]Ibid.

[10]Ibid.

[11]Ibid., p. 3.

[12]*Foreign Relations, 1944*, 5:615.

[13]Amitzur Ilan, "The Conference at Yalta and the Palestine Problem," *Jerusalem Journal of International Relations* (Fall 1977): 37.

[14]*Foreign Relations, 1943*, 4:811–15; *Foreign Relations, 1945*, 8:691.

[15]Ilan, "The Conference at Yalta," p. 40.

[16]Stettinius, *Roosevelt and the Russians*, pp. 72, 278; Leahy, *I Was There*, p. 295; Ilan, "The Conference at Yalta," pp. 34, 44.

[17]Ilan, "The Conference at Yalta," p. 50.

[18]Robert E. Sherwood, *Roosevelt and Hopkins: An Intimate History*, pp. 873–74.

[19]Lord Charles Moran, *Churchill: Taken from the Diaries of Lord Moran: The Struggle for Survival, 1940–1965*, pp. 234, 242–43, 247.

VIII
An Appraisal

As might be expected with a series of agreements that informed the peace so pervasively, and that influenced the origins of the Cold War so directly, the Crimean decisions have drawn the attention over the years of a broad spectrum of journalists, scholars, and politicians. No diplomatic gathering of the twentieth century has received more spirited analysis than the Yalta Conference, and none has evoked as many inadequate assessments.

The terms of evaluation have not always elucidated the right issues. Provoked by right-wing critics, historians have allowed themselves to be drawn into debate over whether President Roosevelt was guilty of national betrayal in giving so much to the Soviet Union. To charges that he gave away the store, either out of sympathy for Soviet interests or naïveté, his supporters have argued that the president operated out of an acute sense of realism at Yalta, and that Alger Hiss, purportedly the mole within the U.S. State Department who engineered the sellout, performed a minor and insignificant function at the conference. A slightly different but related charge has been that Roosevelt was mentally deficient and thus incapable of adequately performing his duties as a negotiator. He surrendered too much to Stalin because he could not comprehend the issues. To this his defenders have responded acerbically that no proof has been adduced of presidential incapacity during the conference, and that Roosevelt's decisions did not diverge significantly from the advice contained in the background papers prepared by the State Department.[1]

Although essentially correct, even the president's defenders often fail to go far enough in their analysis. There is circumstantial evidence that the Soviets in February 1945 saw Hiss, later convicted of perjury for lying about functioning as a Soviet agent in the 1930s, as a reliable source of information, and Soviet Ambassador to the United States Andrei Gromyko later curiously requested that the young State Department employee serve as temporary secretary general of the United Nations.[2] While Hiss had access to all the information pertaining to UN questions, he patently did not perform a sabotaging role at Yalta, nor did he collaborate with the president in any betrayal of American interests. That President Roosevelt suffered from a high degree of mental impairment during the conference now appears beyond dispute; that he was incapable of understanding the implications of his actions, given the help and preparation of his assistants, is not. His failures were generally not those of mental capacity.

Debates over the agreements have paralleled discussion of Roosevelt's performance. Critics have attacked the Polish and Far Eastern settlements as insufficiently attentive to the interests of the Chinese and the Poles and have argued that the arrangements regarding Germany allowed the Soviets to take excessive reparations. Others have countered that the agreements in themselves were more than satisfactory to Western interests, as well as to the Poles and Chinese, but were later repudiated by Stalin. Had the Soviets not broken the accords, they would stand as models of Allied cooperation. A standard supporting thesis, and a strong one as far as it goes, is that the Soviet Union held most of the military cards at Yalta, and thus the agreements simply reflected a realistic assessment of conditions on the part of all the participants.[3]

A more recent interpretation, one put forward by postrevisionist historians of the Cold War, is that Yalta comprised a balance-of-power agreement of the highest order. According to this thesis, President Roosevelt and Prime Minister Churchill recognized that victory over Germany would bring Soviet domination in Eastern Europe, and that the Western allies acknowledged this fact in the agreements over Poland. Stalin, according to this argument, had reason to be surprised when Western leaders later challenged Soviet behavior in that region. Pledges in support of free elections in Poland and the platitudes of the Declaration on Liberated Europe were developed to satisfy public opinion in the United States and Great Britain and were not viewed seriously by either Roosevelt or Churchill. Taking the argument one step further, other historians have averred that a "Yalta system" and Yalta axioms emerged from the Crimean Conference.[4]

That the balance-of-power/Yalta-as-system argument has some validity there is no doubt. It is also true that President

Roosevelt and Prime Minister Churchill expected the democratic provisions they inserted into the agreements to have meaning, and that the West would retain a measure of influence in Eastern Europe. Neither the prime minister nor the president was a cynical realpolitiker, nor was Roosevelt attentive enough in his planning for the conference to cooperate in the erection of a "system." As far as Northeast Asia was concerned, the one area in which Roosevelt attempted to establish a large policy, he expected Stalin's pledge of support for Jiang Jieshi to place limitations on Soviet aspirations. In Manchuria, Chinese Nationalist sovereignty, which Stalin seemed ready to promote, would prove to be an antidote to Soviet expansionism. At the same time, there was no deal consummated to delineate influence in Japan, Korea, or the Pacific region.

The aforementioned terms of evaluation provide some insight into the work of Allied leaders at Yalta, but they do not illuminate enough areas of concern. Additional questions that the historian must answer are whether wartime summit conferences represented the proper forums for the conclusion of Allied agreement; whether summit conferences generally are defensible; whether the West had a chance to gain anything at the Crimean Conference; and, assuming that President Roosevelt knew vaguely what he wanted, whether what he desired could be achieved.

Since the practice has become so commonplace over the past forty years, most readers are aware of the standard arguments in defense of summitry. It is said that the practice allows heads of state to establish personal relationships that would not be possible otherwise and to gain empathy for the essential goals and human aspirations of one another. Once basic understanding begins, the process of settling difficult national disputes is facilitated. Also, talks themselves are good as a sort of catharsis, whether or not the prospect of progress exists. Negotiations cannot hurt, and they might achieve positive results.

Another argument in favor of summit conferences, particularly with Soviet leaders, is that some heads of state really do have controlling power, and, if one wishes to be effective in dealing with authoritarian regimes, it is necessary to go to the top. An unconvincing, but often repeated, corollary assertion is that it is sometimes possible, despite an inability to work out details of an agreement, to achieve a summit-level "agreement in principle." What this usually means is no agreement at all.

All things considered, summit conferences have had serious deficiencies, in both the World War II and contemporary contexts. No American president, not Wilson at Versailles, Roosevelt at Tehran or Yalta, Eisenhower at Geneva, or Kennedy at Vienna, has been well prepared for the give and take of complex negotiation. The president simply does not have the time, except at great cost and at the expense of other matters that must receive his attention, to study the issues at the length or intensity required. It is not sufficient to have the experts along for consultation; in a rough situation the president himself must know the answers. To quote former Secretary of State Dean Rusk, "The principal negotiator must be much more than a mouthpiece for the sheets of paper put in front of him by a staff."[5]

The president of the United States also does not gain very much as a result of personal contact with other statesmen. What he does gain is transitory and easily offset by the problems that a personal exchange may promote. It should go without saying that accidents of personality, assuming the heads of state are compatible, cannot form the basis of any lasting relationship. It should be equally clear that personal hatred and animosity should not be allowed to get in the way of constructive accommodation in which the latter is mutually beneficial.

Unfortunately, a basic fact of summitry is the emphasis on mythmaking and the creation of illusion that emanates from conferences of heads of state. At Yalta, Churchill and Roosevelt were desirous of achieving at least the appearance of cooperation and agreement because they feared that otherwise public opinion in their respective countries would force reactive policies toward the Soviets. Generally, summits promote the international scoreboard mentality in which winning and losing on various points are portrayed by the press in the manner of a supranational athletic event. Moreover, at times the principal players act out their parts more for domestic advantage than for the cause of international tranquility.

By far the most important reason why heads of state should leave difficult negotiations to subordinates is that the latter can explore issues at greater length and more thoroughly. Negotiators can debate various points of view, advance and reject complex propositions, and try out ideas without the commitment of prestige that ensues when heads of state are present. Using a sports metaphor, Dean Acheson has written in his memoirs that, if the president of the United States fumbles the ball, there is no one between him and the goal line. If a subordinate makes a mistake it can be corrected when referred to the head of state.[6]

Assuming the obstacles to successful negotiations inhering in summit conferences, it is possible that certain circumstances make such sessions necessary, and, given the latter assumption, that Yalta may have been one occasion when the Allied leaders simply had to get together. Nothing could be further from the truth. Two questions arise: Was anything achieved at the Crimean meetings that could not have been better accomplished by the foreign ministers? Did the West have much to gain by going to a summit? Stalin did not want a meeting, stating that instead he would send Molotov anywhere in the world. He would trust his subordinate to represent his views faithfully, and he would certainly expect that his allies could do likewise with their foreign secretaries. Careful study of the Yalta decisions suggests that Stalin's instincts were right, and that most of what was done should have been left to the ministers.

Careful study also leads, then, to the conclusion that the conference should not have taken place at all. Logistically, it was extremely difficult to hold, a fact that would have diminished somewhat if it had been held in London, Jerusalem, Athens, or any of the sundry places suggested before the unfortunate choice of the Soviet Black Sea resort. However, arranging a summit, especially in wartime with the transportation and security problems, not to speak of accommodations for several hundred staff people, was still a difficult proposition at best no matter where its location. For President Roosevelt, with his physical infirmities and the rigors of transport, to travel halfway around the world was a mistake of the first order, and one that probably shortened his life. Nor was it an easy trip for Prime Minister Churchill.

It was a conference in which the West had only a marginal chance of success. Tougher negotiating with Lend-Lease and the use of the displaced Soviet citizens as leverage might have achieved some modification of the agreement on Poland. A determination by the United States to avoid purchasing Russian entry into the Pacific war might have brought a more favorable postwar arrangement in Northeast Asia. By the end of 1944 and early 1945, however, the Soviets possessed such a dominant military position in Eastern and Central Europe and, at the same time, such clear-cut objectives for the tier of states on their periphery that it was going to be exceedingly difficult to achieve agreements that were not highly favorable to them. In retrospect it appears, ironically, that only the prime objective of President Roosevelt—cooperation in the establishment of a United Nations—would be possible, and the president, his advisers, and the Western press would grossly overvalue this agreement.

If summit conferences deal in illusion, Yalta epitomized the problems of illusion. Within one year, disillusion became the dominant sentiment in the United States and Great Britain, and, given the circumstances, it could not have been otherwise. Western leaders returned, articulating a litany of praise for Stalin, the Soviet state, the United Nations, and the "new" spirit of cooperation; they hailed the inauguration of a new era. Nothing at Yalta had provided the basis for such optimism.

In evaluating President Roosevelt's role, it is important to note that he knew vaguely what he wanted, although he refused to develop an agenda for the conference, and he stressed the achievement of cooperation with the Soviets as his primary goal. Here the historian must ask whether the latter was any more achievable than was a pro-Western resolution of the critical issues. Despite Roosevelt's vaunted personal charm, there was not much chance, given such obstacles as the absence of a satisfactory state relationship during the period prior to 1941. Certainly nothing in the background of Soviet-American relations recommended cordiality. From American intervention in the Russian civil war, to sixteen years of official nonrecognition, to anti-Bolshevik emotions through the 1920s, U.S. sentiment remained unremittingly hostile. Recognition by Roosevelt in 1933 did little to change the situation. The commercial exchange that the United States hoped for did not materialize because Congress in 1934 enacted legislation making it impossible to extend credit to nations defaulting on their World War I debts. The Soviets, at the same time, refused to restrict their propaganda and subversion efforts, although they had promised to do so in the recognition agreement. They remained bitterly hostile toward both the American system and all capitalist states. Stalin's purges of the late 1930s, and his subsequent nonaggression pact with Hitler, evoked deep revulsion in the United States. Most Americans shared the views of former President Herbert Hoover and then Senator Harry S. Truman that there was not much difference between Hitler's Germany and Stalin's Russia.

Dealing with Stalin's regime during World War II, moreover, did little to inspire trust. The Soviets were secretive, demanding, and singularly unfriendly. They insisted on Lend-Lease support as a right and refused to provide military plans, statements of economic need, or access to Soviet airfields. To expect Stalin to come around given his personal paranoia, not to mention his prejudices and crimes of the previous fifteen years, would have required, to paraphrase William Bullitt, a conversion as dramatic as that of Saul on the road to Damascus. President Roosevelt was not that persuasive.

In negotiating with Stalin at Yalta, Roosevelt was following his interpretation of the requirements of détente, a policy that the president had pursued since the German attack on Russia in June 1941. Several assumptions on the part of U.S. officials predicated this first attempt at détente, which in the final analysis would prove just as ephemeral as the celebrated effort of the 1970s. One assumption was that the mutual objective of defeating Germany, and then Japan, would overcome past differences and allow the United States and the Soviet Union, which would acquire a dominant position on the European continent, to live in relative harmony. Another was that, while the United States would emerge from the war as the world's most powerful nation, its power would be neutralized by traditional isolationist sentiment and the desire to avoid stationing U.S. armies in Europe. The result would be roughly comparable Soviet-American power, a prerequisite to effective détente. President Roosevelt also believed, a belief encouraged by Stalin, who took pains during the war to camouflage his intentions, that ideology would be far less important in the future Soviet-American relationship than it had been in the past. Interest would transcend ideology.

Finally, Roosevelt assumed that he was working with a Soviet leadership that not only was capable of maintaining détente but also was as firmly committed as he to its goals. Given this fact he would have no problem codifying at Yalta the essential feature of détente, which was the mutual and equal desire to maintain an agreed upon postwar status quo.

Unfortunately, the problem with Roosevelt's détente, as later with President Richard Nixon's, was the asymmetry in national goals between the United States and the Soviet Union. Stalin's view of détente was that it should guarantee Soviet wartime and postwar aspirations. This meant Western support in victory over Germany, a British-American stamp of approval on Soviet control of Eastern Europe, and domination of Northeast Asia. It also meant that the Soviets would be free when the emergency ended to resume ideological competition with the West. This included encouraging Communist parties throughout Western Europe to take advantage of unsettled conditions to promote revolution in the democracies. Moreover, it meant trying to gain loans from the United States on highly favorable terms and obtaining access to American military secrets. Finally, because of the need to justify the continuation of the harsh and repressive regime, and to avoid the appearance of weakness, détente meant isolating the Soviet Union and adopting a menacingly aggressive posture toward the rest of the world. A prominent historian of Soviet international relations has written that "détente, in the Kremlin's view was not meant as a sharp break with its traditional policies."[7] His reference was to the 1970s, but it also applies to the 1940s and to Stalin's agreements with the West at Yalta.

Notes

[1]Examples of works sympathetic to Roosevelt include Herbert Feis, *Churchill-Roosevelt-Stalin: The War They Waged and the Peace They Sought*; John L. Snell, ed., *The Meaning of Yalta: Big Three Diplomacy and the New Balance of Power*; Robert Dallek, *Franklin D. Roosevelt and American Foreign Policy, 1932–1945*; and James MacGregor Burns, *Roosevelt: The Soldier of Freedom*. For works critical of Roosevelt's diplomacy at Yalta see William Bullitt, "How We Won the War and Lost the Peace, Part One," *Life* 25, no. 9 (August 30, 1948): 91–94; and William Bullitt, "How We Won the War and Lost the Peace, Part Two," ibid., no. 10 (September 6, 1948): 86–90. Felix Wittmer, *The Yalta Betrayal: Data on the Decline and Fall of Franklin Delano Roosevelt*, is a classic example of the most vituperative and irresponsible journalism. A thorough discussion of Roosevelt's critics, including Westbrook Pegler and George Sokolsky, can be found in Athan G. Theoharis, *The Yalta Myths: An Issue in U.S. Politics, 1945–1955*.

[2]Allen Weinstein, *Perjury: The Hiss-Chambers Case*, pp. 360–61. As Weinstein points out, this must be the only time in history when the Soviets suggested that an American be placed in charge of anything.

[3]For critical assessments of the Polish and Far Eastern settlements at Yalta see John A. Lukacs, *The Great Powers and Eastern Europe*; and Tang Tsou, *America's Failure in China*. Theoharis's *The Yalta Myths* analyzes the views of the critics who denounced the cession of Polish territory. For opposing views supportive of Roosevelt see Snell, *The Meaning of Yalta*; Feis, *Churchill-Roosevelt-Stalin*; Robert E. Sherwood, *Roosevelt and Hopkins: An Intimate History*; Charles E. Bohlen, *Witness to History, 1929–1969*; Lisle Rose, *After Yalta*; and Diane S. Clemens, *Yalta*. The neoconservatism fashionable in the mid-1980s had provoked

new wave of controversy about Yalta. In a September 1985 article in *Commentary*, John Colville, wartime private secretary to Prime Minister Churchill, criticized Roosevelt for the concessions in Eastern Europe, particularly those in Poland. Subsequent essays in the November issue of the same magazine by Lionel Abel, Jeane Kirkpatrick, Robert Nisbet, and Irving Kristol complete the indictment of FDR and his associates. Theodore Draper offered a rebuttal in the *New York Review of Books* which elicited an exchange of views by Lionel Abel, Josef Skvorecky, Robert Nisbet, and Theodore Draper. This debate sheds no new light on the Yalta accords, but it does demonstrate the persistent intense feeling surrounding the conference and its participants. See John Colville, "How the West Lost the Peace in 1945," *Commentary* (September 1985): 41–47; Lionel Abel et al., "How Has the United States Met Its Major Challenges Since 1945?" *Commentary* (November 1985): 25–108; Theodore Draper, "Neoconservative History," *New York Review of Books* (January 16, 1986): 5–15; and Lionel Abel et al., "Neoconservative History: An Exchange," ibid. (April 24, 1986): 49–51.

[4]John Lewis Gaddis, "Was the Truman Doctrine a Real Turning Point?" *Foreign Affairs* (January 1974): 386–402; Daniel Yergin, *Shattered Peace: The Origins of the Cold War and the National Security State*; Akira Iriye, *The Cold War in Asia: A Historical Introduction*.

[5]Dean Rusk, "The President," *Foreign Affairs* (April 1960): 361.

[6]Ibid.; Dean Acheson, *Present at the Creation: My Years in the State Department*, p. 480.

[7]Adam Ulam, "Fifty Years of Troubled Coexistence," *Foreign Affairs* (Fall 1985): 27.

Bibliography

Manuscript Collections

Franklin D. Roosevelt Library, Hyde Park, New York
   Edward J. Flynn Papers
   Harry L. Hopkins Papers
   Henry Morgenthau, Jr., Papers
   Franklin D. Roosevelt Papers
      Map Room File
      Official File
      President's Personal File
      President's Secretary's File
   John G. Winant Papers
University of Oklahoma Library, Norman, Oklahoma
   Patrick J. Hurley Papers

Government Documents

U.S. Department of State. *Foreign Relations of the United States: The Conferences at Malta and Yalta, 1945.* Vol. 8. Washington, DC, 1955.
————. ————: *The Conference at Quebec, 1944.* Washington, DC, 1972.
————. ————: *Diplomatic Papers: The Conference of Berlin (The Potsdam Conference), 1945.* 2 vols. Washington, DC, 1960.
————. ————: *Diplomatic Papers, 1943.* Vol. 4. Washington, DC, 1964.
————. *United States Relations with China with Special Reference to the Period 1944–1949.* Washington, DC, 1949.
U.S. Senate. Committee on Foreign Relations and Committee on Armed Services. *Military Situation in the Far East.* 82d Cong., 1st. sess., 1951.

Micropublications

British Foreign Office: Russia Correspondence, 1941–1945.
   Wilmington, Delaware, 1980.
British Foreign Office: United States Correspondence, 1938–1945.
   Wilmington, Delaware, 1979.

OSS/State Department Intelligence and Research Reports.
  Washington, DC.
U.S. Declassified Documents Reference System. Arlington, Virginia.

Books

Acheson, Dean. *Present at the Creation: My Years in the State Department.*
  New York, 1969.
Adenauer, Konrad. *Memoirs 1945–1953.* Translated by Beate Ruhm von
  Oppen. Chicago, 1965.
Agar, Herbert. *The Price of Power: America Since 1945.* Chicago, 1957.
Alexander, Harold. *The Alexander Memoirs.* London, 1962.
Alliluyeva, Svetlana. *Only One Year.* New York, 1969.
Almond, Gabriel A. *The American People and Foreign Policy.* New York,
  1950.
Alperovitz, Gar. *Atomic Diplomacy: Hiroshima and Potsdam.* New York,
  1950.
Ambrose, Stephen E. *Rise to Globalism: American Foreign Policy Since 1938.*
  London, 1971.
———. *The Supreme Commander.* London, 1971.
Asbell, Bernard. *The F.D.R. Memoirs.* New York, 1973.
Baldwin, Hanson W. *Great Mistakes of the War.* New York, 1949.
Beaumont, Joan. *Comrades in Arms: British Aid to Russia, 1941–1945.* Lon-
  don, 1980.
Bernstein, Barton, and Matusow, Allen, eds. *The Truman Administration:
  A Documentary History.* New York, 1966.
Bethell, Nicholas. *The Last Secret.* New York, 1974.
Bialer, Seweryn, ed. *Stalin and His Generals.* New York, 1969.
Birse, A. H. *Memoirs of an Interpreter.* New York, 1967.
Bishop, Jim. *FDR's Last Year: April 1944–April 1945.* New York, 1974.
Blum, John Morton. *From the Morgenthau Diaries: Years of Crisis, 1928–
  1938.* Boston, 1959.
———. *From the Morgenthau Diaries: Years of War, 1941–1945.* Boston,
  1967.
———. *Roosevelt and Morgenthau: (A Revision and Condensation of) From
  the Morgenthau Diaries.* Boston, 1970.
———. *V Was for Victory: Politics and American Culture During World
  War II.* New York, 1976.
———, ed. *The Price of Vision: The Diary of Henry A. Wallace.* Boston,
  1973.
Bohlen, Charles E. *The Transformation of American Foreign Policy.* New
  York, 1969.
———. *Witness to History, 1929–1969.* New York, 1973.
Bryant, Arthur. *Triumph in the West, 1943–1946.* London, 1959.

Buhite, Russell D. *Patrick J. Hurley and American Foreign Policy*. Ithaca, New York, 1973.
————. *Soviet-American Relations in Asia, 1945–1954*. Norman, Oklahoma, 1981.
Burnham, James. *Containment or Liberation? An Inquiry into the Aims of United States Foreign Policy*. New York, 1952.
Burns, James MacGregor. *Roosevelt: The Soldier of Freedom*. New York, 1970.
Byrnes, James F. *Speaking Frankly*. New York, 1958.
Campbell, Thomas M., and Herring, George C., eds. *The Diaries of Edward R. Stettinius, Jr., 1943–1946*. New York, 1975.
Carr, Albert A. *Truman, Stalin, and Peace*. Garden City, New York, 1950.
Carr, Robert K. *The House Committee on Un-American Activities, 1945–1950*. Ithaca, New York, 1952.
Chamberlain, William Henry. *Beyond Containment*. Chicago, 1953.
Churchill, Winston, S. *Closing the Ring*. Boston, 1951.
————. *The Second World War*. 6 vols. Boston, 1948–1953.
Ciechanowski, Jan. *Defeat in Victory*. New York, 1947.
Clay, Lucius D. *Decision in Germany*. Garden City, New York, 1950.
Clemens, Diane S. *Yalta*. New York, 1970.
Crocker, George N. *Roosevelt's Road to Russia*. Chicago, 1959.
Dallek, Robert. *Franklin D. Roosevelt and American Foreign Policy, 1932–1945*. New York, 1979.
Dallin, Alexander. *German Rule in Russia*. New York, 1957.
Davis, Lynn Etheridge. *The Cold War Begins: Soviet-American Conflict Over Eastern Europe*. Princeton, 1974.
Davison, W. Phillips. *The Berlin Blockade*. Princeton, 1958.
Deane, John R. *The Strange Alliance: The Story of Our Efforts at Wartime Cooperation with Russia*. New York, 1947.
Dennett, Raymond, and Johnson, Joseph E. *Negotiation with the Russians*. Boston, 1951.
DeSantis, Hugh. *The Diplomacy of Silence: The American Foreign Service, the Soviet Union, and the Cold War, 1933–1947*. Chicago, 1980.
Deutscher, Isaac. *Stalin: A Political Biography*. Rev. ed. London, 1966.
Dilks, David, ed. *The Diaries of Sir Alexander Cadogan, 1938–1945*. New York, 1972.
Djilas, Milovan. *Conversations with Stalin*. Translated by Michael B. Petrovich. London, 1969.
Donovan, Frank. *Mr. Roosevelt's Four Freedoms: The Story Behind the United Nations Charter*. New York, 1966.
Dulles, John Foster. *War or Peace*. New York, 1950.
Eddy, William. *F.D.R. Meets Ibn Saud*. New York, 1954.
Eden, Anthony. *The Eden Memoirs*. Vol. 2, *The Reckoning*. London, 1965.
Elliot, Mark R. *Pawns of Yalta: Soviet Refugees and America's Role in Their Repatriation*. Urbana, Illinois, 1982.

Erickson, John. *The Road to Berlin: Continuing the History of Stalin's War with Germany*. Boulder, Colorado, 1983.

Eubank, Keith. *The Summit Conferences, 1919–1960*. Norman, Oklahoma, 1966.

Feis, Herbert. *The China Tangle: The American Effort in China from Pearl Harbor to the Marshall Mission*. Princeton, 1953.

————. *Churchill-Roosevelt-Stalin: The War They Waged and the Peace They Sought*. Princeton, 1957.

Fenno, Richard F., Jr., ed. *The Yalta Conference*. Lexington, Massachusetts, 1972.

Fisher, Harold H. *America and Russia and the World Community*. Claremont, 1946.

Fleming, Denna W. *The Cold War and Its Origins 1917–1960*. 2 vols. Garden City, New York, 1961.

Flynn, Edward J. *You're the Boss*. New York, 1947.

Fontaine, André. *History of the Cold War*. Vol. 1. Translated by D. D. Paige. New York, 1968.

Friedel, Frank. *FDR: Launching the New Deal*. Boston, 1973.

Gaddis, John Lewis. *Russia, the Soviet Union, and the United States: An Interpretive History*. New York, 1978.

————. The United States and the Origins of the Cold War. New York, 1972.

Galbraith, John Kenneth. *A Life in Our Times: Memoirs*. Boston, 1981.

Gallagher, Hugh Gregory. *FDR's Splendid Deception*. New York, 1985.

Gardner, Lloyd C. *Architects of Illusion*. Chicago, 1972.

Gardner, Lloyd C.; Schlesinger, Arthur, Jr.; and Morgenthau, Hans J. *The Origins of the Cold War*. Waltham, Massachusetts, 1970.

Gilbert, Martin. *Churchill*. Garden City, New York, 1980.

————. *Did Churchill Have a Political Philosophy?* New York, 1981.

————. *Winston Churchill, the Wilderness Years*. Boston, 1982.

Goldberg, Richard Thayer. *The Making of Franklin D. Roosevelt: Triumph over Disability*. Cambridge, Massachusetts, 1981.

Goldman, Eric. *The Crucial Decade: America, 1945–1955*. New York, 1956.

Graebner, Norman. *The New Isolationism*. New York, 1958.

Grey, Ian. *Stalin: Man of History*. Garden City, New York, 1979.

Halle, Louis. *The Cold War as History*. New York, 1967.

Harriman, W. A., and Abel, E. *Special Envoy to Churchill and Stalin*. London, 1976.

Hassett, William D. *Off the Record with F.D.R., 1942–1945*. New Brunswick, New Jersey, 1958.

Herring, George. *Aid to Russia, 1941–1946*. New York, 1973.

Herz, Martin. *Beginnings of the Cold War*. Bloomington, Indiana, 1966.

Hewlett, Richard G., and Anderson, Oscar E., Jr. *The New World: 1939–46*. University Park, Pennsylvania, 1962.

Higgins, Trumbull. *Soft Underbelly: The Anglo-American Controversy over the Italian Campaign, 1939–1945*. New York, 1968.

Horowitz, David. *The Free World Colossus*. New York, 1965.
Hull, Cordell. *The Memoirs of Cordell Hull*. 2 vols. New York, 1948.
Hutton, J. Bernard. *Stalin—The Miraculous Georgian*. London, 1961.
Hyde, H. Montgomery. *Stalin: The History of a Dictator*. New York, 1971.
Iriye, Akira. *The Cold War in Asia: A Historical Introduction*. Englewood Cliffs, New Jersey, 1974.
Ismay, Lord. *Memoirs*. 2 vols. London, 1960.
Israelian, Victor. *The Anti-Hitler Coalition: Diplomatic Cooperation Between the USSR, USA, and Britain During the Second World War, 1941–1945*. Moscow, 1971.
Jackson, J. Hampden. *The World in the Postwar Decade 1945–1955*. Boston, 1956.
Jones, Robert Huhn. *The Roads to Russia: United States Lend Lease to the Soviet Union*. Norman, Oklahoma, 1969.
Jowitt, Earl. *The Strange Case of Alger Hiss*. New York, 1953.
Kacewicz, George V. *Great Britain, the Soviet Union and the Polish Government in Exile (1939–1945)*. The Hague, 1979.
Kaiser, Robert G. *Cold Winter, Cold War*. New York, 1974.
Kennan, George F. *Memoirs*. Vol. 1, *1925–1950*. New York, 1969.
Kimball, Warren F., ed. *Churchill & Roosevelt*. Vol. 3, *The Complete Correspondence*. Princeton, 1984.
————, ed. *Franklin D. Roosevelt and the World Crisis, 1937–1945*. Lexington, Massachusetts, 1973.
————. *Swords or Ploughshares? The Morgenthau Plan for Defeated Nazi Germany, 1943–1946*. Philadelphia, 1976.
King, F. P. *The New Internationalism: Allied Policy and the European Peace 1939–1945*. Hamden, Connecticut, 1973.
Kolko, Gabriel. *The Politics of War*. New York, 1969.
Kuklick, Bruce. *American Policy and the Division of Germany*. Ithaca, New York, 1972.
Kuniholm, Bruce R. *The Origins of the Cold War in the Near East: Great Power Conflict and Diplomacy in Iran, Turkey, and Greece*. Princeton, 1980.
Kuter, Lawrence S. *Airman at Yalta*. New York, 1955.
LaFeber, Walter. *America, Russia, and the Cold War, 1945–1966*. New York, 1980.
Lane, Arthur Bliss. *I Saw Poland Betrayed: An American Ambassador Reports to the American People*. New York, 1948.
Leahy, William D. *I Was There: The Personal Story of the Chief of Staff to Presidents Roosevelt and Truman Based on His Notes and Diaries Made at the Time*. New York, 1950.
L'Etang, Hugh. *The Pathology of Leadership*. New York, 1970.
Leuchtenburg, William E., ed. *Franklin D. Roosevelt: A Profile*. New York, 1967.
Levering, Ralph B. *American Opinion and the Russian Alliance, 1939–1945*. Chapel Hill, 1976.

Liddell-Hart, B. H. *The History of the Second World War*. New York, 1971.
Loewenheim, Francis L., et al. *Roosevelt and Churchill: Their Secret Wartime Correspondence*. New York, 1975.
Lucas, Richard C. *The Strange Allies: The United States and Poland, 1941–1945*. Knoxville, Tennessee, 1978.
Lukacs, John A. *The Great Powers and Eastern Europe*. New York, 1953.
————. *1945: Year Zero*. New York, 1978.
Macmillan, Harold. *The Blast of War, 1939–1945*. New York, 1968.
Maisky, Ivan. *Memoirs of a Soviet Ambassador*. New York, 1968.
Manchester, William. *The Last Lion, Winston Spencer Churchill: Visions of Glory, 1874–1932*. Boston, 1983.
Matray, James Irving. *The Reluctant Crusade: American Foreign Policy in Korea, 1941–1950*. Honolulu, 1985.
May, Gary. *China Scapegoat: The Diplomatic Ordeal of John Carter Vincent*. Washington, DC, 1979.
McCagg, William O., Jr. *Stalin Embattled, 1943–1948*. Detroit, 1978.
McNeill, William H. *America, Britain, and Russia: Their Cooperation and Conflict, 1941–1946*. London, 1953.
Merli, Frank J., and Wilson, Theodore A. *Makers of American Diplomacy: From Theodore Roosevelt to Henry Kissinger*. New York, 1974.
Mikolajczyk, Stanislaw. *The Pattern of Soviet Domination*. New York, 1948.
————. *The Rape of Poland: Pattern of Soviet Aggression*. New York, 1948.
Millis, Walter, ed. *The Forrestal Diaries*. New York, 1951.
Moran, Lord Charles. *Churchill: Taken from the Diaries of Lord Moran: The Struggle for Survival, 1940–1965*. Boston, 1966.
Morray, J. P. *From Yalta to Disarmament*. New York, 1952.
Mosely, Philip E. *The Kremlin and World Politics*. New York, 1960.
Neumann, William L. *After Victory: Churchill, Roosevelt, Stalin and the Making of the Peace*. New York, 1967.
————. *Making the Peace, 1941–1945*. Washington, DC, 1950.
Notter, Harley, ed. *Postwar Foreign Policy Preparation, 1939–1945*. Washington, DC, 1949.
O'Conor, John F. *Cold War and Liberation: A Challenge of Aid to the Subject Peoples*. New York, 1961.
Patterson, James T. *Mr. Republican: A Biography of Robert A. Taft*. Boston, 1972.
Pelling, Henry. *Winston Churchill*. New York, 1974.
Penrose, E. F. *Economic Planning for the Peace*. Princeton, 1953.
Perkins, Frances. *The Roosevelt I Knew*. New York, 1946.
Pogue, Forrest C. *George C. Marshall: Organizer of Victory, 1943–1945*. New York, 1973.
Ponomaryov, B.; Gromyko, A.; and Khvostow, V., eds. *History of Soviet Foreign Policy, 1917–1945*. Moscow, 1969.
Radosh, Ronald. *American Labor and United States Foreign Policy*. New York, 1969.
Range, Willard. *Franklin D. Roosevelt's World Order*. Athens, Georgia, 1959.

st the Peace in 1945." *Commentary*

History." *New York Review of Books*

Homework." *Saturday Review* (July 8,

: A Reassessment." *Foreign Affairs*

e a Real Turning Point?" *Foreign*

eration with the Soviet Union—A
arren F. Kimball, ed., *Franklin D.*
7–1945. Lexington, Massachusetts,

alta." *South Atlantic Quarterly* (Octo-

oosevelt: The Patrician as Oppor-
burg, ed., *Franklin D. Roosevelt: A*

Yalta and the Palestine Problem."
elations (Fall 1977): 28–52.
of the Lublin Government." *Slavonic*
72): 410–33.
a." *Congressional Record*, vol. 93, pt.

Iran, 1941–1947: The Origins of
gazine of History 59 (Autumn 1975):

Eastern Europe and the Origins of
lternative Interpretation," *Journal*
981): 313–36.
s, the Soviet Union, and the Far
Historical Review (May 1955): 153–

onference, 4–11 February 1945."
e Yalta Conference. Lexington, Mas-

'Yalta.'" *Saturday Review* (April 16,

ground of the Yalta Agreements."
21.
e War with Japan." *Foreign Affairs*

t of Germany: The Allied Negoti-
oreign Affairs (April 1950): 487–98.
any: New Light on How the Zones
uly 1950): 580–604.

Redvers, Opie and Associates. *The Search for Peace Settlements*. Washington, DC, 1951.
Rees, David. *Harry Dexter White: A Study in Paradox*. New York, 1973.
Reilly, Michael F. *Reilly of the White House*. New York, 1947.
Rhode, Gotthold, and Wagner, Wolfgang, eds. *The Genesis of the Oder-Neisse Line in the Diplomatic Negotiations During World War II: Sources and Documents*. Stuttgart, Germany, 1959.
Rigby, T. H., ed. *Stalin*. Englewood Cliffs, New Jersey, 1966.
Rodine, Floyd H. *Yalta: Responsibility and Response, January–March 1945*. Lawrence, Kansas, 1974.
Roosevelt, Eleanor. *This I Remember*. New York, 1949.
Roosevelt, Elliott. *As He Saw It*. New York, 1946.
———, ed. *F.D.R.: His Personal Letters, 1928–1945*. Vol. 2. New York, 1950.
Roosevelt, Elliott, and Brough, James. *A Rendezvous with Destiny: The Roosevelts of the White House*. New York, 1975.
Rose, Lisle A. *After Yalta: America and the Origins of the Cold War*. New York, 1973.
Rosenman, Samuel I., ed. *The Public Papers and Addresses of Franklin D. Roosevelt*. Vol. 12, *The Tide Turns, 1943*. New York, 1950.
———, ed. *The Public Papers and Addresses of Franklin D. Roosevelt*. Vol. 13, *Victory and the Threshold of Peace, 1944–1945*. New York, 1950.
———. *Working With Roosevelt*. New York, 1952.
Rothwell, Victor. *Britain and the Cold War, 1941–1947*. London, 1982.
Rovere, Richard H. *Senator Joe McCarthy*. New York, 1959.
Rozek, Edward J. *Allied Wartime Diplomacy: A Pattern in Poland*. New York, 1958.
Russell, Ruth B. *A History of the United Nations Charter: The Role of the United States, 1940–1945*. Washington, DC, 1958.
Sainsbury, Keith. *The Turning Point: Roosevelt, Stalin, Churchill, and Chiang Kai-shek, 1943: The Moscow, Cairo, and Teheran Conferences*. New York, 1985.
Seton-Watson, Hugh. *The East European Revolution*. 3d ed. New York, 1956.
Sherwood, Robert E. *Roosevelt and Hopkins: An Intimate History*. Rev. ed. New York, 1952.
Smith, Gaddis. *American Diplomacy During the Second World War, 1941–1945*. New York, 1965.
Smith, Walter Bedell. *My Three Years in Moscow*. Philadelphia, 1950.
Snell, John L., ed. *The Meaning of Yalta: Big Three Diplomacy and the New Balance of Power*. Baton Rouge, 1955.
———. *Wartime Origins of the Dilemma Over Germany*. New Orleans, 1959.
Standley, William H., and Ageton, Arthur A. *Admiral Ambassador to Russia*. Chicago, 1955.
Stettinius, Edward R., Jr. *Roosevelt and the Russians: The Yalta Conference*. Edited by Walter Johnson. Garden City, New York, 1949.

Stimson, Henry L., and Bundy, McGeorge. *On Active Service in Peace and War*. New York, 1947.

Stoler, Mark. *The Politics of the Second Front*. Westport, Connecticut, 1977.

Sulzberger, C. L. *A Long Row of Candles: Memoirs and Diaries, 1934–54*. New York, 1969.

Taft, Robert A. *A Foreign Policy for Americans*. New York, 1951.

Taubman, William. *Stalin's American Policy: From Entente to Détente to Cold War*. New York, 1982.

Theoharis, Athan G. *The Yalta Myths: An Issue in U.S. Politics, 1945–1955*. Columbia, Missouri, 1970.

Thorne, Christopher. *The Limits of Foreign Policy*. New York, 1973.

Townley, Ralph. *The United Nations: A View From Within*. New York, 1968.

Trukhanovsky, L. *British Foreign Policy in the Second World War*. Moscow, 1969.

Truman, Harry S. *Memoirs*. 2 vols. Garden City, New York, 1955–56.

Tsou, Tang. *America's Failure in China*. Chicago, 1963.

Tucker, Robert C. *Stalin as Revolutionary, 1879–1929: A Study in History and Personality*. New York, 1973.

Tucker, Robert W. *The Radical Left and American Foreign Policy*. Baltimore, 1971.

Tugwell, Rexford G. *The Democratic Roosevelt: A Biography of Franklin D. Roosevelt*. Reprint ed. Baltimore, 1969.

Ulam, Adam B. *Expansion and Coexistence: The History of Soviet Foreign Policy 1917–67*. New York, 1968.

———. *The Rivals: America and Russia Since World War II*. New York, 1971.

———. *Stalin: The Man and His Era*. New York, 1973.

Walton, Richard J. *Henry Wallace, Harry Truman, and the Cold War*. New York, 1976.

Warburg, Paul. *Germany—Bridge or Battleground*. New York, 1946.

Weinstein, Allen. *Perjury: The Hiss-Chambers Case*. New York, 1978.

Werth, Alexander. *Russia at War*. London, 1964.

Westerfield, H. Bradford. *Foreign Policy and Party Politics: Pearl Harbor to Korea*. New Haven, 1955.

Wheeler-Bennett, J., ed. *Action This Day*. London, 1968.

Wheeler-Bennett, John, and Nicholls, Anthony. *The Semblance of Peace*. New York, 1972.

Widenor, William C. *Henry Cabot Lodge and the Search for an American Foreign Policy*. Berkeley, 1980.

Williams, William Appleman. *American-Russian Relations, 1781–1947*. New York, 1952.

———. *The Tragedy of American Diplomacy*. Rev. ed. New York, 1962.

Wilmot, Chester. *The Struggle for Europe*. New York, 1952.

Colville, John. "How the West Lo (September 1985): 41–47.

Draper, Theodore. "Neoconservativ (January 16, 1986): 5–15.

Field, Henry. "How F.D.R. Did His 1961): 8–10.

Gaddis, John Lewis. "Containmen (July 1977): 873–88.

———. "Was the Truman Doctri *Affairs* (January 1974): 386–402.

Gardner, Lloyd C. "FDR and Coor Policy of Procrastination." In W *Roosevelt and the World Crisis, 193* 1973.

Hammer, Oscar J. "The 'Ashes' of Y ber 1954): 477–84.

Hofstadter, Richard. "Franklin D. tunist." In William E. Leuchter *Profile*. New York, 1967.

Ilan, Amitzur. "The Conference at *Jerusalem Journal of International R*

Janczewski, George H. "The Origin *and East European Review* (July 19

Lindley, Ernest. "Roosevelt at Yalt 14:4226.

Mark, Eduard. "Allied Relations i a Cold War Crisis." *Wisconsin Ma* 51–63.

———. "American Policy Toward the Cold War, 1941–1946: An *of American History* (September 1

May, Ernest R. "The United Stat Eastern War, 1941–1945." *Pacifi* 74.

McNeill, William H. "The Yalta In Richard F. Fenno, Jr., ed., *T* sachusetts, 1972.

Millis, Walter. "From 'Argonaut' t 1955): 24–25.

Morton, Louis. "The Military Bac *The Reporter* (April 7, 1955): 19–

———. "Soviet Intervention in th (July 1962): 653–62.

Mosely, Philip E. "Dismembermer ators from Yalta to Potsdam." *I*

———. "The Occupation of Germ Were Drawn." *Foreign Affairs* (J

Pan, Stephen C. Y. "Legal Aspects of the Yalta Agreement." *American Journal of International Law* (January 1952): 40–59.

Parzen, Herbert. "The Roosevelt Palestine Policy, 1943–1945: An Exercise in Dual Diplomacy." *American Jewish Archives* (April 1974): 31–65.

Rusk, Dean. "The President." *Foreign Affairs* (April 1960): 353–69.

Sokolosky, George. "Crime of Yalta." *Congressional Record*, 81st Cong., 1st sess., p. A-2072.

Sontag, Raymond J. "Reflections on the Yalta Papers." *Foreign Affairs* (July 1955): 615–23.

Ulam, Adam. "Fifty Years of Troubled Coexistence." *Foreign Affairs* (Fall 1985): 27.

Warner, Geoffrey. "From Teheran to Yalta: Reflections on F.D.R.'s Foreign Policy." *International Affairs* (July 1967): 530–36.

White, P. J. "New Light on Yalta." *Far Eastern Survey* (1950): 105–12.

Winnacker, Rudolf A. "Yalta—Another Munich?" *Virginia Quarterly Review* (Autumn 1948): 521–37.

Zacharias, Ellis M. "The Inside Story of Yalta." *United Nations' World* (January 1949): 12–17.

Other Unpublished Material

Carroee, David. "The Yalta Conference." Master's thesis, Columbia University, 1962.

Haska, Lukas E., Jr. "Summit Diplomacy During World War II: The Conferences at Teheran, Yalta, and Potsdam." Ph.D. dissertation, University of Maryland, 1966.

Walker, Gregg B. "Franklin D. Roosevelt as Summit Negotiator at Teheran, 1943 and Yalta, 1945." Ph.D. dissertation, University of Kansas, 1983.

Yaung, Emily. "The Impact of the Yalta Agreement on China's Domestic Politics, 1945–1946." Ph.D. dissertation, Kent State University, 1979.

Index